The Mega Church

How To Make Your Church Grow

Second Edition

DAG HEWARD-MILLS

Parchment House

Unless otherwise stated, all Scripture quotations are taken from the
King James Version of the Bible

THE MEGA CHURCH (2ND EDITION)
HOW TO MAKE YOUR CHURCH GROW

Copyright © 1999, 2011 Dag Heward-Mills

First Edition published by Parchment House 1999
Published by Lux Verbi.BM (Pty) Ltd. 2008
8th Printing 2008

Second Edition published by Parchment House 2011
16th Printing 2020

⁷⁷Find out more about Dag Heward-Mills at:

Healing Jesus Campaign
Write to: evangelist@daghewardmills.org
Website: www.daghewardmills.org
Facebook: Dag Heward-Mills
Twitter: @EvangelistDag

ISBN : 978-9988-8501-0-4

Contents

Contents

CHAPTER 1

Twenty-Five Reasons Why You Must Have a Mega Church

1. **You must desire to have a mega church because that is the most appropriate vision and goal for a pastor.** The best vision and burning desire for every pastor is the vision for a large church. Why not have a large church if you are going to have a church?

   Where there is no vision, the people perish: but he that keepeth the law, happy is he.

   Proverbs 29:18

2. **You must desire to have a mega church because the desire for a mega church will lead you on a journey that will make your church grow.** Having a desire for miracles will lead to the specific result of having miracles in your ministry. Having a desire for the anointing will lead to the specific result of having the anointing. The desire for church growth will lead you on a journey of discovery that will make your church grow.

   Therefore I say unto you, what things soever ye desire, when ye pray, believe that ye receive them, and ye shall have them.

   Mark 11:24

1

3. **You must have a mega church because the prophetic destiny of every church that the Lord builds is to have a greater end than the beginning.** Do not be discouraged about the smallness of your church today. It has been predicted that the end of your ministry will be much more glorious than the beginning.

Because the word of God prophesies that the glory of the latter house shall be greater than the glory of the former, you must expect something more glorious than what you saw at the beginning. God will do something great and He will increase the congregation.

Though thy beginning was small, yet thy latter end should greatly increase.

Job 8:7

4. **You must have a mega church because most pastors are deceived into thinking that the work is being done when it is not being done.**

During the time of His ministry, Jesus made a very important statement.

...The harvest truly is plenteous, but the labourers are few...

Matthew 9:37

This means there are plenty of winnable souls. There is plenty of work for us all. There are plenty of people to fill our churches.

Many pastors are deceived by the fact that their little halls are full. Many ministers feel that they have "arrived" in ministry. You receive a nice salary and have a nice car. God has blessed you and all your expenses are paid for. This does not mean that you have "arrived". Do not let the devil blind your eyes to the real work we have to do. It is Satan who fans the church to sleep!! He whispers to the hearts of many ministers: "Everything is O.K." "This is it." "You have made it." "This is how far you can go." "This is everything you can achieve for God!" Such ministers have had their spiritual and visionary eyes blinded by Satan. The enemy whispers to their heart, "Everything is okay. This is it! You have made it!"

Satan wants your church to remain small. The fewer people you have in your congregation the more captives he has. The size of your church shows you to what extent you are depopulating Hell. When you have a megachurch, it means that you are establishing more souls. It also means that more souls have escaped from the clutches of the devil.

5. **You must have a mega church because God's will is that "His house may be filled." Most churches are not filled because they are not mega churches.**

> And the lord said unto the servant, Go out into the highways and hedges, and compel them to come in, THAT MY HOUSE MAY BE FILLED.
>
> Luke 14:23

In Luke 14, the Lord gave us an important revelation. The master said to his servant, "I need my house to be filled." The master in this story represents Jesus. Jesus wanted His house to be filled. In other words, Jesus wants His churches to be filled. God wants full churches! The master in this story was not content with having just a few people at his party. He could have had the party anyway, but he wanted many more people. And more especially he wanted the house to be filled.

Through this story, God is showing His will for the church. His will is more people! His will is filled rooms! His will is overflowing churches! His will is the MEGACHURCH!

6. **You must have a mega church because your harvest field is the world.**

> **God did not send us to a suburb of your town. Neither did He send us to a few villages. He sent us to the whole world. If we had a small field to harvest from, then we could not expect a large quantity of harvested fruits.**

And he said unto them, Go ye into all the world, and preach the gospel to every creature. He that believeth and is baptized shall be saved; but he that believeth not shall be damned.

Mark 16:15-16

The fact that the entire world is to be reached implies that the harvest of souls that we will bring in must be very large. It will definitely be a major portion of the world's population. If a major section of the world's population is to be saved through the preaching of the gospel, then every church should be bursting at the seams for lack of space. Remember that there are over six billion souls out there waiting for us to reach them with the Gospel.

7. **You must have a mega church because the biblical example of churches had thousands of members.** Is the early church not the best example for us to follow? If the early church had three thousand and five thousand people, should these numbers not serve as a guiding post for us? Indeed, these numbers are recorded in the bible so that we may know what to aim for.

Those who believed what Peter said were baptized and added to the church--about three thousand in all. They joined with the other believers and devoted themselves to the apostles' teaching and fellowship, sharing in the Lord's Supper and in prayer.

Acts 2:41-42 (NLT)

But many of the people who heard their message believed it, so that the number of believers totaled about five thousand men, not counting women and children.

Acts 4:4 (NLT)

8. **You must have a mega church because having a large church means that more souls have been won to the kingdom.** In a large church there will be more services,

more altar calls and more opportunities to be saved than a small church. Is it not the aim of every minister of the gospel to win souls to the Lord? Is it not an extra added blessing that a mega church leads to the salvation of many people who join it?

9. **You must have a mega church because in a mega church more workers and labourers are released to work for God.**

He said to his disciples, "The harvest is so great, but the workers are so few. So pray to the Lord who is in charge of the harvest; ask him to send out more workers for his fields

Matthew 9:37-38 (NLT)

There will always be a certain percentage of the flock who are real labourers. No matter what you do or say, a certain percentage of the church will not get involved in the real work of ministry. There will always be the spectators and observers. There will always be the commentators. The labourers will always be in the ministry. The larger the crowd you have, the more labourers will be sent forth. And the more easily you will be able to finance them.

10. **You must have a mega church because through a mega church more ministers of the gospel, full time pastors and bishops are appointed and released into the harvest field.** In a large church there is always a training programme that produces ministers. A ten thousand member congregation will therefore produce more pastors than a hundred member church. Indeed, the pastor of a smaller church is not likely to have enough people who want to be ministers of the gospel.

11. **You must have a mega church because in a mega church more people are involved in prayer against the power of the prince of the air.**

For we wrestle not against flesh and blood, but against principalities, against powers, against the rulers of the darkness of this world, against spiritual wickedness in high places.

Wherefore take unto you the whole armour of God, that ye may be able to withstand in the evil day, and having done all, to stand.

Stand therefore, having your loins girt about with truth, and having on the breastplate of righteousness;

And your feet shod with the preparation of the gospel of peace; Above all, taking the shield of faith, wherewith ye shall be able to quench all the fiery darts of the wicked. And take the helmet of salvation, and the sword of the Spirit, which is the word of God:

Praying always with all prayer and supplication in the Spirit, and watching thereunto with all perseverance and supplication for all saints

Ephesians 6:12-18

When you have a megachurch, more prayer will go forth unto the Lord. Therefore, more people will be saved and established. When the Lord sent me to establish churches in Europe, He showed one key role that we were going to play in rebuilding His kingdom in that continent. You see, Europe has virtually become a continent of atheists. They have put God out of their minds. Many Europeans do not believe that God even exists.

Years ago, Europe sent out missionaries to the world. But now, they have fallen to the lowest state of demonic blindness and godlessness. The Lord showed me that one of our duties as a church was to release prayer into the atmosphere concerning the Church in Europe. Our presence in countries like Switzerland, The Netherlands and England, has resulted in much more intercession being made in those nations.

Our church in Geneva has all-night prayer meetings every Friday, praying from midnight until 6 a.m. They engage in spiritual warfare in a land where God is forgotten. As more churches like ours go into the nations, then more prayer will take place. This is one of the primary reasons why a large and branching church is important.

When the church I pastor, The Lighthouse Cathedral, grew to a certain size, we were able to successfully have all-night prayer meetings everyday. We had so many small groups within the church that it was possible to set up a rotation so that one of these groups could have an all-night prayer meeting everyday. Thus, we had a different group praying every night.

The larger the church, the more prayer groups are created. More prayer is possible in a megachurch! That is why the devil wants the church to remain small!

12. **You must have a mega church because a mega church generates large crowds and large crowds create great expectation.**

And as the people were in expectation, and all men mused in their hearts of John, whether he were the Christ, or not.

Luke 3:15

Through experience I have noticed that the larger the crowd, the greater the expectation. When there is a large gathering of God's people, there is an air of excitement, expectation and real faith. Why is this? This happens because the faith of everyone is heightened by what they see.

The sight of a large crowd inspires faith and creates excitement. The combined faith of the crowd is greater than the faith of just one person. That helps to draw out the gift of God from the minister.

I have preached to small groups and to very large crowds. The spiritual atmosphere of these two situations is often different.

13. **You must have a mega church because in a mega church you will have a greater manifestation of miracles because of the greater crowds and greater expectation.**

Then Philip went down to the city of Samaria, and preached Christ unto them. And the people with one accord gave heed unto those things which Philip spake, hearing and seeing the miracles which he did. For unclean

7

spirits, crying with loud voice, came out of many that were possessed with them: and many taken with palsies, and that were lame, were healed. And there was great joy in that city.

Acts 8:5-8

And they went forth, and preached every where, the Lord working with them, and confirming the word with signs following.

Mark 16:20

Whenever there is great faith, you can expect more power and miracles of healing. Jesus often said, "Your faith has made you whole." It is faith that generates the miraculous! I know some people will misunderstand me on this. I am not saying that God does not move in small congregations. I often minister in small congregations, and I see God moving in a wonderful way. God certainly does miracles in small churches. All I am saying is that, generally speaking, when there are more people, there is more faith, more expectation and therefore, more miracles. I think even the simplest Christian can understand this simple logic.

A bigger church means more people, which means more faith, which means more power, which means more miracles, which results in more testimonies!

Don't you want more glory, power and anointing to flow in your congregation? Dear pastor friend, believe God for a bigger church. With a bigger church, many more blessings will flow from the throne of God to his people.

14. **You must have a mega church because more evangelism is possible through a mega church.**

And now the word of the Lord is ringing out from you to people everywhere, even beyond Greece, for wherever we go we find people telling us about your faith in God. We don't need to tell them about it,

1 Thessalonians 1:8 (NLT)

One of the side effects of having a larger church is that more evangelism takes place. Our Cathedral is divided into about fifteen chapels. Under each chapel, there are several ministries and under each ministry several fellowships.

It is our policy that every ministry has at least one major outreach during each month. Since our church has many ministries, it is possible that fifty different outreaches by fifty different groups will be taking place at the same time at many different locations!

More soul winning has taken place simply because the church has grown larger. It is God's will for your church to grow larger so that more souls will be won for the Lord.

15. **You must have a mega church because a mega church has a larger and greater income that can be used for the work of God.**

> Neither was there any among them that lacked: for as many as were possessors of lands or houses sold them, and brought the prices of the things that were sold, and laid them down at the apostles' feet: and distribution was made unto every man according as he had need.
>
> Acts 4:34-35

Having more people also means having a higher church income. If a church has a good pastor, the money of the church will be used for the right things. Unfortunately, some pastors are more like vampires – they suck the blood of the church rather than pour their lives into the ministry.

A higher income means many more spiritual goals are achievable. Money is not an evil thing. Money is neutral! It is the love of money that is evil! Money is a weapon in the hand of man. If a good man has money he will use it to do good things. A good minister will use the income of a mega church to build the church and promote the gospel!

I had a dream that we would one day have trucks driving around the nation, holding crusades in every town and village. Once upon a time, that was just a dream. Now, with a larger church we have been able to purchase a truck and have begun crusading all across the nation. How was that possible? We had more people and therefore more money, and we could do more for God!

16. **You must have a mega church because special ministries which take care of special needs will develop within a mega church.**

It is important to desire to have a large church. Pastors must dream of having large congregations. A large church results in the multiplicity of many ministries. It results in the multiplication of several important activities in the church. For instance, it multiplies the ministry of music.

Initially, our church had only one choir. Now we have no less than six choirs in addition to numerous other singing groups. What does this mean? It means that a large church has resulted in vital multiplication. It is the will of God that more of His children sing for Him. The more singing groups we have, the more God is glorified. The number of choirs you have depends on the number of people in the church.

As the church grows, it becomes more diverse in its composition. This results in specialist ministries being developed. When you have a small church, there will usually be very few special ministries like a ministry to the poor, refugees, and to orphans. As the church becomes larger it is possible to get involved in some of these other areas. When a church is able to be involved in these special areas, many blessings are released! Look at the blessings that are available to churches that minister to the poor.

Blessed is he that considereth the poor: the Lord will deliver him in time of trouble. The Lord will preserve him, and keep him alive; and he shall be blessed upon the earth: and thou wilt not deliver him unto the will of his enemies.

Psalm 41:1, 2

These are powerful blessings for those who are able to grow to the point where they minister to special needs. Often when a church is small, it does not have the capacity to reach out in these areas. Have a vision of building a megachurch. Other special areas of ministry will develop within it. You will have people with the ministry of giving being released. There are churches which have men and women with a heart for financing the gospel.

...he that giveth, let him do it with simplicity;

Romans 12:8

It is rare to come across church members who have the ability to make a difference in the church through their giving. Every pastor would love to have members who take care of major expenses for the church.

In the earlier stages of our church's life, I had no one who could do things like that. But now, there are people who have the ability and the ministry of giving.

Other special areas that can develop are ministries to the poor and to the disabled. I have a dream to establish an orphanage. I've had this dream for a long time. But, it will take a large and strong church to be able to support such a venture. If you have a hundred orphans in your orphanage, you have to pay for three hundred meals a day. You also have to buy clothes for a hundred people. You then have to pay the hospital bills for a hundred children. After that you have to pay several professionals to care for these motherless and fatherless people. I think that you will agree with me that it will take a truly megachurch to set up such a ministry.

17. **You must have a mega church because it shows that you have made full proof of your ministry.** Many ministers do not do a thorough job of being pastors! Many ministers

11

only touch the surface of their calling! Many ministers are a phantom of what they could be! Most churches have the potential of growing larger. Often, the growth does not come because the pastor does not do a thorough job of pastoring the church. Every field of endeavour has greater or lesser dimensions. You must aim for the greatest possible dimension in pastoral work.

But you – keep your eye on what you are doing; accept the hard times along with the good; keep the Message alive; do a thorough job as God's servant.

2 Timothy 4:5 (The Message)

18. **You must have a mega church because in a mega church there are more "beloveds" (potential marriage partners).**

For there was not a needy person among them, for all who were owners of land or houses would sell them and bring the proceeds of the sales

Acts 4:34 (NASB)

Years ago, when our church was much smaller, a young lady said to me, "My type of man is not in this church." When I looked throughout my congregation, I realized that what she said was true. There was no suitable person for this woman to marry. Some years later she went ahead and married an unbeliever.

At another point another lady said, "There is no man who is old enough to marry me. So I'm going to a larger church where I can find a man to marry me." You see, she was thirty-nine years old and there were no forty-year-old bachelors in the church. All of the bachelors we had in our church were in their twenties and thirties. In a mega church there are brides and grooms of all ages. In a megachurch, even people over the age of seventy can become bridegrooms and brides.

19. **You must have a mega church because in a mega church more marriages and more weddings take place.**

People love to get married in church. Marriages and weddings are a spicy blessing for every congregation. The congregation always loves to hear of the announcement of upcoming marriages. They get excited and hope and pray that it will be their turn soon. You will be blessed with more weddings when you have a mega church. A healthy growing church is one that has numerous marriages taking place. I always pray that there will be more weddings and marriages in my church.

20. **You must have a mega church because there are more contacts and connections through the people in the mega church.**

   As we have therefore opportunity, let us do good unto all men, especially unto them who are of the household of faith."

   Galatians 6:10

   The larger the church the more contacts and "connections" can be made. Let's face it, many things in this world depend on "who you know!" You may get a breakthrough just because you belong to a certain church. I have employers in my church to whom I can recommend potential employees. When our church was smaller, it was only full of students. Now, many people can find jobs through the church.

   People like to stay in a place that has added blessings and security. The church members love these fringe benefits of making contacts and connections with others.

21. **You must have a mega church because in a mega church there is always a large pool of employers who can help the church members.** In a large church you will have more people who are substantial enough to provide jobs to help the congregation. In a mega church you will have the added benefit of being able to fight the scourge of unemployment in your congregation.

   And the congregation of those who believed were of one heart and soul; and not one of them claimed that anything belonging to him was his own; but all things were common property to them.

13

And with great power the apostles were giving witness to the resurrection of the Lord Jesus, and abundant grace was upon them all. For there was not a needy person among them, for all who were owners of land or houses would sell them and bring the proceeds of the sales

Acts 4:32-34 (NASB)

22. **You must have a mega church because all the different needs of the congregation can be met through the mega church.** A congregation is a group of people with varied needs. When I stand before large crowds asking them to lay hands where they have a need, everyone prays fervently because everyone has a need. If there are a thousand people, there are a thousand different needs. A mega church affords you the chance to meet many of these different needs. If there is a small church and someone needs a lawyer's advice it is not likely that he will find one. But in a large church, you are likely to find a lawyer, a doctor, an engineer, a pharmacist or even a psychiatrist.

And all those who had believed were together, and had all things in common; and they began selling their property and possessions, and were sharing them with all, as anyone might have need.

Acts 2:44-45 (NASB)

23. **You must have a mega church because a mega church is more likely to accomplish the 25% biblical quota of souls won from the community.**

And when he sowed, some [25%] seeds fell by the way side... some [25%] fell upon stony places... some [25%] fell among thorns... But other [25%] fell into good ground and brought forth fruit...

Matthew 13:4-8

The Bible teaches us that the sower went out to sow the Word of God in a city. The result was that, one out of four (25%) of his seeds yielded good results. If we win only a quarter of our cities to Christ, I can assure you that there will be no more half-filled churches.

It is time for the Church to achieve its biblical quota of twenty- five percent of the population. How many people are there in your city?

There are about four million people in the city of Accra, Ghana. According to my little theory, at least twenty-five percent of them should have responded to the Word of God. This means that at least one million of these people should be safely established in the Church. However, I wonder how many people darken the doorways of church buildings in Accra every Sunday morning. Several thousands do, but I doubt whether it reaches our biblical quota of twenty-five percent of the population.

If the church of God attains the twenty-five percent goal, there will be many many large churches scattered all over the city. Every church will have multiple church services from morning to evening. Calculate it for yourself! You will see that the Church is no where near attaining that twenty-five percent goal. How many born again Christians attend church on a Sunday morning in your city? What is the population of your city?

Total citywide born again church attendance = 25% ??

Total population of your city

When I did this calculation for my own city, I realized that we were far from achieving the results of that "sower who went out to sow". But I prophesy that churches shall be filled in the last days. The land shall be filled with megachurches. God wants big churches because He is expecting at least twenty-five percent of the population to respond positively to our preaching.

24. **You must have a mega church because a mega church is a force to reckon with and it becomes a nation within a nation.**

As the church increases in size it will become a powerful community. It virtually becomes a nation of its own. Governments begin to fear the power and influence of a mega church, but they despise small churches. Governments know that a large church means a lot of people, which means a lot of votes. The politicians fear the power of the masses. They know that popular opinion keeps them in power. They know that pastors are influencing people's minds. Small things are easy to despise. The Bible says,

For who hath despised the day of small things?

Zechariah 4:10

Politicians can no longer despise the reality of the Kingdom of God when it is massive! They cannot attack the pastors in the churches when they know the number of people they lead.

Our church was once attacked and the walls around us broken. The people behind the attack thought that they could get away with it easily. They did not appreciate the magnitude, strength and scope of influence of the church they were attacking. The "people behind the scenes" were very surprised when the attack led to a nationwide crisis. Several churches and the general public rallied together against the perceived attackers. The politicians had to act quickly to prevent nationwide demonstrations and civil unrest.

As you read this book, I want you to believe God for a megachurch. I want you to receive the anointing to rise out of smallness into the largeness that God has destined for you.

25. **You must have a mega church because the glory of the end time church will be greater than the glory of the early church.**

The glory of this latter house shall be greater than of the former, saith the Lord of hosts...

Haggai 2:9

The Bible predicts that the glory, which means beauty, of the latter day church, will far exceed the glory of the former one. I believe that we are in that latter day. When I consider what the Lord has done in Ghana over the last fifteen years, I realize that God is bringing a greater glory to His end-time Church. The largest churches some fifteen years ago would be the youth groups of some of the megachurches that God has raised up today!

Let me share with you a very important secret. God does not work with only one person. The Spirit of God does not move in only one church. If a pastor has been able to achieve great growth in your city, it is a clear sign that the grace of God is abundant for the work of church growth there.

People who think that God is only using one man are deceived!

The Lord ministered powerfully to Ahab the king through Elijah the Tishbite (1 Kings 17, 18, 21). But there was another powerful prophet called Micaiah who was used to rebuke Ahab the king. God does not limit Himself to one man.

Elijah made the mistake of thinking he was the only one who was faithful to God.

> And he said, I have been very jealous for the Lord God of hosts: because the children of Israel have forsaken thy covenant, thrown down thine altars, and slain thy prophets with the sword; and I, even I only, am left...
>
> 1 Kings 19:14

But the Lord showed him that He had seven thousand other faithful prophets.

> Yet I have left me seven thousand in Israel, all the knees which have not bowed unto Baal, and every mouth which hath not kissed him.
>
> 1 Kings 19:18

Many big churches are springing up. God is raising up men and women of integrity to pastor His people. Flow in it. Catch the spirit! You will also walk in the glory of the latter church. Learn the strategies of church growth. Obtain the power and the wisdom of God. Walk in love towards the brethren. Love even those who slander and betray you. Every great work of the Holy Spirit is as a result of love, unity and teamwork.

I really want to emphasize and stress this great truth that God does not work with one isolated person. Did you know that when Ezekiel was prophesying between 622-600 B.C., Daniel the prophet was also raised up and prophesied between 616-536 B.C.

It was a time when God was moving through great prophets – people who yielded themselves to the call were used greatly in the ministry. Interestingly enough, Jeremiah also ministered between 685-616 B.C. You will notice that the time periods often overlap. This is because the Spirit of God does great works with many people at the same time.

Isaiah (792-722 B.C.), Nahum (786-757 B.C.) and Micah (772-722 B.C.) were raised up in the ministry around the same period of time. You must buy into the move of God when the season comes. Zechariah and Malachi both prophesied about the end-times. Their ministries, interestingly enough, spanned the same period of time 557-525 B.C.

What am I trying to say? I am showing you that God is using many people to do the same thing in a particular season. He is building megachurches now! Jump on the train and become the pastor that God wants you to be. Did you know that God moved in a spirit of reform during the sixteenth century? Did you know that He did not only work through Martin Luther in Germany?

At the time the spirit of reform was flowing through the ministry of Martin Luther, the spirit of reform was also flowing through a man called Zwingli in Switzerland. If Martin Luther had thought he was the only anointed reformist he would have been making a big mistake! God moves in waves! There is a wave of church growth right now. There is a wave of massive harvesting of souls! Get in on this move of God! Allow God to use you to build a megachurch!

Be open to learn new things that you do not know. A common statement in my church is, "You don't know everything! You and I are learning. Everyday of our lives should be a living classroom. Everyone you meet can teach you something!"

As we study the subject of church growth through the power and wisdom of God, decide that you can do it. Do not let the failures of yesteryear keep you down. Be a "Can-do man". Rise up in your spirit and say, "We are able to possess the land. We can do it!"

...Let us go up at once, and possess it; for we are well able to overcome it.

Numbers 13:30

When you say, "I can," the Holy Spirit will rise up to perform that which He has called you to do. Remember, you did not call yourself. Faithful is He that called you and He will do it. You are the believer and God is the doer.

I remember when our church had only one member that owned a car – me! I prayed that we would have more people in our church with cars. I confessed and believed that we had ten people in our church who owned cars. After some time, I received what I believed God for. Believe that the God who called you, will do it.

Faithful is he that CALLETH you, who also will DO it.

1 Thessalonians 5:24

I recall walking up and down the streets adjacent to the canteen we had rented for our church services. I spoke to the street and said, "Be filled with cars." I spoke to the empty benches and said, "Be filled with members." Today there are countless numbers of cars and members in our church.

CHAPTER 2

How to Measure Church Growth

If you read the back of this book, you will realize that I did not specify how many members I have in my church. There is an important reason for this. I believe in real numbers and I have learnt that many people count the same thing differently! If I gave you a number of the members in my church, you may not know exactly how I arrived at that figure. Consequently, I may end up giving you the wrong impression.

It is important for the credibility of pastors that we say what we mean and mean what we say. I used to get confused by the numbers that certain pastors claimed to have in their churches.

I have visited these churches at night and counted the chairs in their halls (I am an expert at counting chairs quickly). I would ponder, "How can they claim to have so many thousand members in their church?"However, as I checked and rechecked the number of chairs, I realized that there was no way that those numbers could be accurate. Even with the addition of canopies and multiple services, there was no way that I could correlate the numbers that I heard with what I had actually seen. Maybe they were counting all the people who were present in spirit, but not in the flesh. After all, Paul claimed that he attended the Corinthian church in spirit.

For I verily, as absent in body, but present in spirit...

1 Corinthians 5:3

I could not bring myself to believe that the pastors were telling lies. I prefer to think that they were just counting in a different way. I realize that there are different ways of counting. There are seven types of counting that I have observed in the Body of Christ. And I think it will do us all some good to know which type of counting is being used.

7 Types of Counting

1. Type 1 counting

'Type 1 counting,' is the counting of the number of human beings *physically present at a particular meeting.* It is the headcount of people in *attendance.* This is the headcount. **I believe this type of counting is the most informative of all the types of counting.** However, it is probably the least used way of counting because it is usually the lowest!

When I ask my data officer for numbers in the church, I get the *Type 1* numbers. I need to know the *Type 1* figures. I work best with *Type 1 Counting.* The fact is that only a fraction of your members come to church on Sundays. If you use the *Type 1 Counting*, you are only talking about a fraction of the real number of people that God has given you to look after. In spite of this, I still prefer to work with *Type 1 Counting* because it provokes me to work harder.

2. Type 2 counting

This is the total number of people on the church register. Many churches quote this *Type 2* number as their membership. The *Type 2* Counting is larger or smaller depending on how far back the church will go in counting its registered members. The figure also depends on whether the church updates or revises its

21

membership lists frequently. It also depends on *how* a church revises the membership list. Some churches have what we call 'active members'.

For some people, an active member is someone who attends a service at least once a month. For others it is someone who attends every Sunday service. I consider an active member to be someone who comes to church during the week, i.e., not only on Sundays. For others it is someone who belongs to a smaller cell group.

All of these can vary the eventual outcome of the *Type 2 Counting*. What this means is that my ten thousand figure may be different from your ten thousand figure. **That is why I prefer to stay with Type 1 Counting because there can be no variation in the method of counting heads who are actually present.**

Some pastors give a *Type 2* figure as their regular attendance. When you attend their church and see the actual number of people, you may be very disappointed.

There is often a sharp contrast between the number of people physically present and the number of people the pastor claims to be his members. You may even think the pastor has a problem with lying or exaggeration.

I have seen situations where the *Type 1* Counting is as low as ten percent of what they claim to be their membership. The church may claim to have ten thousand members, but only one or two thousand are present in the service.

3. Type 3 counting

This type of counting is often used during conventions and crusades that run over a few days. *It is the cumulative count.* The total number of people who attend the meetings is counted. For instance they could say that the convention was very successful and that, ten thousand people were in attendance.

What they actually mean is that two thousand people came each night for five days! This type of counting is often misleading, as it does not give an accurate picture of the truth.

4. Type 4 counting

This is where the seating capacity of the building is used to estimate membership. Sometimes a building has a maximum capacity of three thousand. During a programme, the pastor could say that there were three thousand people in church. This is because the whole church looked full, so the assumption was that three thousand people were there. This is a wrong assumption.

A *Type 1 Counting* could have easily revealed that only two thousand people were present. A hall, that is capable of seating three thousand people, can "look" full when only two thousand people are present. Once again, this is why I feel that *Type 1 Counting* will help us all to know where we are and where we need to go.

5. Type 5 counting

This is when pastors give rough estimates. They try to give a reasonable assessment of the crowd. The pastor thinks he can assess the numbers present in the crowd. He makes estimates based on experience, and concludes for instance that there are about three hundred people present. Sometimes these rough estimations are quite accurate but at other times they can be totally misleading.

The pastor of the local church is likely to give a higher *Type 5 Counting* than the pastor of a sister church who is visiting and observing. The local pastor would say, "There are about two thousand people present." The visiting minister would say, "I think there are about one thousand two hundred people present." The visiting minister would not like his rival's church to look too big, so his figure would therefore be much more modest.

6. Type 6 counting

Type 6 Counting is what I call 'wild and unreasonable guessing'. Some years ago when we had about eight hundred people attending our church, I met someone in London who told me, "I heard you had a convention and there were seven thousand people present."

I asked him, "Who told you that?" He gave me the name of the woman who had said that.

She had said, "I was in the meeting myself and there were about seven thousand people present."

I always wondered "How did she get the figure 'seven thousand'?" She must have had a shot at Type 6 Counting – wild guessing!

7. Type 7 counting

This type of counting aims at outdoing everyone else. A pastor mentions a figure that is higher than any other figure being mentioned in town. If the largest church in town is said to be around five thousand, he will always have around six or seven thousand members. This pastor is suffering from the spirit of lying and exaggeration.

Is it Scriptural to Count?

We need to ask ourselves – is all of this counting biblical? Is it scriptural to be concerned about numbers? Should we not be concerned about quality and not quantity? The answer is implicit throughout the Scriptures.

Numbering was done in the Old Testament. There is an entire book in the Bible dedicated to numbering – the Book of Numbers. In that book, the number of people, the number of soldiers and the number of tribesmen were recorded.

However, there was a time when God was angry with King David because he had numbered the people. It is clear from this that when numbering is done for the wrong reason it displeases God. For instance, if you put your faith and trust in your numbers, you are making a grave mistake.

...for there is no restraint to the Lord to save by many or by few.

1 Samuel 14:6

God will pull down whatever you put your trust in. He wants you to have your faith in Him and Him alone.

In the New Testament, different reports of numbering were mentioned. Everyone knows that Jesus had only twelve disciples. We know that Jesus sent out seventy disciples. It was reported that Jesus appeared to *five hundred people* after He rose from the dead. We also know that *one hundred and twenty* people were waiting for the Holy Spirit in the Upper Room. The Book of Acts records that Peter ministered to *three thousand* people at one time. At another time, we know that *five thousand* responded to an altar call at Peter's crusade.

If these numbers were not important, then why were they recorded in the Bible? **God through the Holy Spirit was teaching us that the numbers of people involved in any spiritual event is a significant indicator.** The numbers are important. The Bible says that God will reward us for the quality of work we have done.

Every man's work shall be made manifest... of what sort it is.

1 Corinthians 3:13

But Luke 19 shows us that God will judge us for how much we have done in His name.

...A certain nobleman went into a far country...when he was returned, having received the kingdom... then he commanded these servants to be called unto him, to

whom he had given the money, that he might know how much every man had gained by trading.

Luke 19:12, 15

God is interested in what sort of work you are doing. But He is also interested in how much.

3 Dangers of Counting

1. The pressure to impress, lie and exaggerate

Many pastors are under pressure to say things that sound impressive. If everyone around you claims to have so many thousand members, you can look foolish if you just have a few hundred. It's almost as though you have not been called by God. *God is not going to reward us because of the number of people in our churches. He is going to reward us for our faithfulness to Him.*

I once attended a convention of a great church. I counted all the people that were seated there. As I said, I have become an expert at counting seats and human beings very quickly. There were a few thousand people present. Later, I heard a claim from the pastor who had held that meeting, that several thousand people had attended the meeting. This pastor was probably under the pressure to impress and to exaggerate. I was there myself! I counted the human beings present, personally. Yet I heard a figure for that meeting which was several times more than the facts.

Perhaps the other thousands were present in spirit. If the people you are counting are there in spirit, please tell us so that we stop looking for them in the physical!!

2. Self-deception and complacency

It is easy to deceive yourself if you use the wrong counting method. I heard one minister say, "The whole area outside the building was full." He continued, "People were sitting under canopies."

That is how he knew that things were getting better. But that is deception. I have learnt not to trust this type of counting. I don't want to be self-deceived. I want to know the reality. When you are self-deceived, you think you are what you are not! You think of yourself more highly than you ought to, but this will lead to your downfall.

...to every man that is among you, not to think of himself more highly than he ought to think...

Romans 12:3

3. Discouragement

You can also be discouraged when you count too often. Counting should be done so that you have a baseline figure you can use as a reference point. This will help you to know whether things have gotten any better over the months.

However, if you want to put on weight, for example, I would not advise you to weigh yourself everyday. You will become depressed because you will not notice any change. Growth should not be and cannot be measured so frequently.

Church attendance can fluctuate so much that following it on a weekly basis can lead to a weakening of the pastor's heart. I have the head usher or data officer in my church do a *Type 1 Counting* every Sunday. But I only ask for the figures after several months have passed. This helps me to see if there is any improvement.

4 Advantages of Numbering

1. Numbering lets you know where you are.

When you know where you are, you can more readily plan your future. (When you know where you are, you know where you want to go.) It helps you to see the reality of what you are doing. It is easy to deceive yourself. Checking the true numbers will help you to move forward with God.

2. Numbering helps to check backsliding.

There is a law of degeneration at work in this world. Everything starts to decay the moment you take your eyes off it. The Bible teaches that you should look diligently to know the state of the flock.

Be thou diligent to know the state of thy flocks, and look well to thy herds. For riches are not for ever...

Proverbs 27:23, 24

Numbering is a diligent way of knowing the state of the flocks. When you are fed with information that things are decaying, you will sit up! When you are stimulated by the veritable facts, it generates a greater vision within you to do God's work. It makes you rise up to build the Kingdom of God.

One day I asked my data officer to tell me the attendance for that Sunday. He told me how many people were in attendance on that day. I was very discouraged because I thought it was a very small number after all my years of hard work. However, when he added the total number of satellite and branch churches, the real fruit of the ministry became clearer to me and I was a bit more encouraged. I decided to start more churches and press on for more growth in the central church.

3. Numbering stimulates growth and generates a new vision and compassion for the lost.

You become dissatisfied with smallness. It leads you to pray. Knowing the true number of people in my ministry has always made me pray more, fast more and seek God more often. You know that prayer changes things, and prayer can change those ugly numbers.

4. Numbering the sheep has been a valuable tool for me to help monitor the increase and decrease of the church.

It will guide you when you need to emphasize on visitation and when you need to judge yourself in areas that may be hindering growth.

Fourteen Important Numbers

There are some important figures that every pastor must always be constantly aware of. Each of these figures has some significance. I have discovered that each meeting has its special role to play in the life and development of the church.

1. The number of people physically present on Sunday mornings (Type 1 Counting of Sunday service)

This number is only a percentage of your true membership. In a normal church a large number of people are absent on some Sundays. This is why the number can fluctuate so much. The Sunday service attendance is the best number to use for monitoring progress in a general way.

2. The number of people present at a weekday service

This tells you the number of the very committed members you have. Most serious Christians make time to attend church during the week. You will find that the anointing and flow of the Spirit is different on a weekday service. A corporate anointing manifests because of the gathering of faithful ones. Lukewarm and religious attendees do not dilute the atmosphere.

3. The number of people present at small group or fellowship meetings

This number shows you how developed the internal structure of the ministry is. There are some churches which can command thousands of people for a special convention, however they are not able to mobilize fifty people on a regular basis for small group meetings. It is important to have these small groups so that they can meet the needs of the members at a personal level.

4. The number of people who attend fasting and prayer sessions

This tells you the number of spiritual soldiers you have. This is very different from the swelled up convention attendance. It should be the goal of every pastor to build up a large core of spiritual warriors. These people may be more dependable.

5. The number of people at a convention

The convention crowd contains many people who are moved by excitement. There are many "miracle seekers" and "sign watchers" in attendance.

6. The number of people absent at each church service

This is a very important number. It tells you how many people are falling away. It is probably an indication of how hard the pastors and shepherds are working. Perhaps they are not being prayed for and they are not being visited.

7. The number of people in the choir of the church

The choir of a church is like the flower of a plant. It is often the part of the church that the outside world sees. It is often a reflection of the organizational skills of the church. It tells us how well the pastors are making use of the talents within the congregation.

8. The number of people in the city where your church is located

A church's size is always related to the size of the city in which it is situated. The largest churches in the world are found in the largest cities in the world. For example, if 0.1 % of people in Accra (a city of 4 million) are in the Lighthouse; then our church population would have to be four thousand. If the membership shoots up to six thousand, we would still form only 0.15% of the population. This figure makes us relatively insignificant.

The figure must be determined every year for us to know how great an impact we are making in the city. If this percentage is insignificant, it must motivate us to have more visitations, more prayer, more fasting and more witnessing. It means that we must have more pastors, more shepherds, more churches, more ministries and more fellowships. We must invite more people, do more follow-up, have more crusades and release more power.

9. The number of people who give their lives to Christ every Sunday

This tells you how conscious of lost souls the pastor is. It shows you whether members are inviting non-Christians to church. It tells us whether the church is fulfilling the Great Commission in getting people born again.

10. The percentage of people who were saved in the church

Occasionally, it is interesting to find out how many people got saved in the church. This tells you how original the church is. Many of my members were saved at the Lighthouse Cathedral. Some churches are made up of breakaway members of other churches. Since this was the source of the majority of their members, they often don't know how to win souls for themselves. Every church must know how to intentionally win souls and assimilate new converts.

11. The number of new converts who are still in the church after two months

This tells you whether follow-up is being done.

12. The number of lay workers in the church

This shows you how involved the general congregation is in the ministry. It tells you what percentage of the church is asleep. *When a human being is asleep only eight percent of his body is at work. If only eight percent of your members are active, it means your church is asleep.*

13. The number of people who pay tithes

This is a reflection of the number of truly loyal people you have. The Bible says, "For where your treasure is, there will your heart be also." It tells you how many people in the crowd have their hearts solidly planted in the church.

14. The number of people who attend the 31st December night service

Traditionally, this is a very well attended service. From my experience, it is the best attended service in the whole year. Superstitious people run to the church so that God will see them in church as the new year dawns. All of those you haven't seen throughout the year may finally show up on 31st December. The pastor is usually encouraged by the 31st December crowd. This swollen number usually regularizes within a few weeks.

CHAPTER 3

How You Can Receive the Anointing

...Not by might, nor by power, but by my spirit, saith the Lord of hosts.

Zechariah 4:6

One thing all of us must realize is that ministry is different from any other secular job. In the secular world, many things are important for success. Zerubbabel was trying to build the temple. We are trying to build the Church. Building the church and building the temple are one and the same thing. The instruction that applied to Zerubbabel applies to us.

The Bible is making it clear that it is not by any form of power that the Church will be built. **The Church will be built by the power of the Holy Spirit** – *end of story!*

Some people who look at me and say, "Oh, he's succeeding because he's educated." But it is not by the power of education. There are educated people in the ministry whose churches have not amounted to a "hill of beans". It is not by education, it is by the anointing.

The Handsome Pastor

I read a newspaper article which said, "The pastor of the church is so handsome. That is why so many young ladies go there." But I know that there are pastors who are not handsome per se, whose ministries have grown into thousands.

Still others say, "Oh, it is their background." "Oh, it is the location of the church." "Oh, it is the wealth of the members." "Oh, it is the exciting music." "Oh, it is the instrumentalists." Everybody tries to give a reason why something does or does not work. There are pastors who have said to me, "You have the strategies!" They think I have loads of hidden tactics to make my ministry work. Some people think I am an expert administrator, that is how come things are working.

In this chapter, I will introduce you to the most important factor that will make you start out and accomplish something substantial for God. I believe in education. I believe in administration. I believe in strategies. But above all, I have come to the conclusion that the Prophet Zechariah came to – *it is not by any form of might, it is not by any power, it is by my Spirit says the Lord.*

This Spirit is the same thing as the anointing. The Bible says in Acts 10:38, "How God anointed Jesus of Nazareth with the Holy Ghost and with power." You will see from this Scripture that the substance that God anointed Jesus Christ with, was the Holy Spirit. Therefore, we can conclude that the anointing is the Holy Spirit.

We need the anointing to do the work.

The ministry is not a human or natural thing. As soon as all ministers get that in their minds, the better it will be for them. When you see a successful minister, look beyond the physical and see into the realm of the spirit. Observe the anointing at work. There is an invisible cloak over that person which allows him to succeed at what he is doing. That invisible mantle is what I call the anointing. It explains why some people succeed and some don't. It explains why some people have greater degrees of success under exactly the same circumstances.

A pastor cannot oversee a very large church, unless he is anointed to do so. I have been in the ministry for nearly twenty years and I know from the Word and by experience that it is by the anointing and nothing else! Jesus told Pilate that all the power he possessed was what God had allowed him to have. Nobody can have power unless God gives it to him.

...Thou couldest have no power at all against me, except it were given thee from above...

John 19:11

I believe that God selects people and specifically anoints them to accomplish certain purposes. When I look back on my life, I can see that I was specifically anointed to do what I'm doing. This is different from a genuine in-filling of the Holy Spirit which every Christian has. Since the anointing is so important, we must ask ourselves, "How do we get this vital ingredient?"

It is very important to realize that the anointing is not *taught* **it is** *caught.* How does this special ingredient come onto a person? Is it something that we can all have or is it reserved

35

for the special few? God is the one who introduces the anointing into the earth. He does it in His own sovereign way. I have noticed different ways by which the anointing is released on the earth.

8 Different Ways the Anointing Is Released

1. Terminated transferred anointing

In this type of transfer, a man of God's life is terminated and his anointing is transferred to someone else. The person who has received the anointing usually starts ministering after the death of the originally anointed vessel. A good example of this is Joshua. Joshua became anointed to lead the people of Israel after Moses' life was terminated.

A transferred anointing is something that is moved from one person to another. **This transfer can occur when a man of God dies or leaves the scene. His mantle then falls directly on someone else.** The departure of Elijah from the scene resulted in the anointing on his life being transferred to Elisha. This resulted in the same anointing being present on the earth, but operating through another human being.

God is concerned about finishing His work and will use which ever vessel is available. I call this *terminated transfer* because death terminates the life and ministry of one man and the anointing is transferred to another. This also happened under the ministry of Jesus. As soon as Christ was off the scene, the anointing that operated through Him whilst He was on earth began to function through His disciples. People were amazed. The only explanation that they could give for Peter and John's new charisma, was their association with Christ.

Now when they saw the boldness of Peter and John,... they marvelled; and they took knowledge of them, that they had been with Jesus.

Acts 4:13

2. Living transferred anointing

The next type of transfer is *living transferred anointing.* **In this case, the anointing on one person is transferred to someone else whilst that man of God is alive.** A man of God who is blessed with long life may see the anointing that is on his life working through others.

For example, the anointing departed from Saul and was replaced by an evil spirit. Meanwhile, his successor, David, was anointed while Saul was alive. Saul saw the anointing to be king on another man and was afraid of him. **This is a common occurrence in the ministry.** Even the Prophet Samuel was afraid to anoint David while Saul was yet alive. He knew that it would provoke much jealousy and hatred.

> **And the Lord said unto Samuel... fill thine horn with oil, and go, I will send thee to Jesse the Bethlehemite: for I have provided me a king among his sons. And Samuel said, How can I go? if Saul hear it, he will kill me...**
>
> **1 Samuel 16:1, 2**

Some older men of God can see that their anointing has left them and moved on to another person. This sometimes leads the older man of God to fight the new one upon whom he sees the anointing. Have you not seen this in your city? The older and insecure men of God fight to keep their position, whilst God works through others. God allowed Saul to fight David in order to test David's character. All things do work together for good to them that are called.

3. Anointing sharing

This is when God takes the anointing on one man and shares it with several other people at the same time. You will notice several men of God in the same era, operating in a similar way. In Bible times, several of the prophets lived and prophesied around the same time. God took of the anointing that was upon Moses and shared it amongst seventy people.

37

...Gather unto me seventy men... and I will take of the spirit which is upon thee, and will put it upon them...

Numbers 11:16, 17

All seventy men were anointed. They shared in Moses' anointing and accomplished God's will. I have seen the anointing on my life being shared to many of my pastors. I can see them operating under the same anointing. I have watched them catch the anointing.

4. Modified anointing transfer

The next type of anointing transfer is what I call a *modified anointing transfer.* **In this case, the anointing is transferred from one individual to another but in the process, it is modified.** In such a case, the recipient of the anointing may be notably different in ministry from the one from whom the anointing was transferred. An example of this can be seen under the ministry of Moses and Joshua. It was Moses who laid hands on Joshua and imparted the Spirit (anointing).

And Joshua the son of Nun was full of the spirit of wisdom; for Moses had laid his hands upon him...

Deuteronomy 34:9

Basically, Joshua was anointed to do battle and take over new lands. Moses did not conquer any new lands, however you could see a similarity between Moses and Joshua. Joshua crossed the River Jordan using the "Red Sea crossing anointing" which he had received from Moses. He ruled the people with the authority of Moses. But apart from this and a few other occurrences, Joshua was quite different from Moses.

5. Diminishing anointing transfer

The *diminishing anointing transfer* occurs when the anointing from one is passed to another, but is reduced in its strength and glory. It is often God's way of fading out a particular ministry.

You will see a clear example of this under the ministries of King David and King Solomon. David's kingly anointing was transferred to his son Solomon and then to Rehoboam and Jeroboam. Solomon's sons did not have the grace of God on their lives to rule over all of the twelve tribes of Israel. We cannot even remember the names of the other kings who lived after Solomon.

This is because the kingly anointing was fading as the years passed by. God showed Solomon before he died, that the anointing on his son Rehoboam would be greatly diminished.

But I will take the kingdom out of his son's [Rehoboam] hand, and will give it unto thee, even ten tribes. And unto his son will I give one tribe...

1 Kings 11:35, 36

Some American universities started out as Christian institutions with a Christian vision. Today, there is not even a trace of Christianity in some of those colleges. The initial anointing is diminished!

6.   Enhanced anointing transfer

This is when the anointing transfer from one person to the other is upgraded. For example, Elisha had twice as much of the anointing that Elijah had and performed twice as many miracles. This type of anointing transfer is unusual. You will notice that Elijah told Elisha that he had asked for a hard thing; that is, to have an *enhanced anointing transfer.*

...Thou hast asked a hard thing...

2 Kings 2:10

7.   Former anointing reintroduced

This type of anointing transfer can be seen in the case of John the Baptist and Elijah. God decided to reintroduce the *Elijah anointing* through a man called John the Baptist. This is because

God was doing a work, which needed a dramatic Elijah-type of ministry.

And if ye will receive it, this [John] is Elias, which was for to come.

Matthew 11:14

I believe that some of the apostolic and prophetic anointings of the early Church are being reintroduced into the Church at this time.

There is therefore a resurgence of the miraculous and the prophetic. There are much more larger churches with ministers preaching to three thousand and five thousand members like Peter did in the Book of Acts.

The Bible predicts that two prophets with a peculiar anointing will arise in the Last Days to challenge the Anti-christ. The Bible says that these two prophets will do certain things. A closer look at the ministry of these two Latter Day prophets reveals a great similarity between their anointings and those of Moses and Elijah. *Once again, this is the principle of the reintroduced anointing at work.*

These two prophets will have power to call down fire from heaven. They will also have power over the weather to prevent it from raining for three and a half years. This sounds very much like Elijah. The Bible also says that they will have power to turn water into blood and command plagues to appear at random. Once again this sounds like the anointing that was on Moses.

And I will give power unto my two witnesses, and they shall prophesy a thousand two hundred and threescore days, clothed in sack cloth. These are the two olive trees, and the two candlesticks standing before the God of the earth. And if any man will hurt them, fire proceedeth out of their mouth, and devoureth their enemies: and if any man will hurt them, he must in this manner be killed. These have power to shut heaven,

that it rain not in the days of their prophecy: and have power over waters to turn them to blood, and to smite the earth with all plagues, as often as they will.

Revelation 11:3-6

Once again, it looks like God is reintroducing a former anointing in order to do a vital job. **The anointing on Moses' life was introduced to fight against a despotic and repressive Pharaoh. The anointing on Elijah's life contended with one of Israel's most detestable and incorrigible kings, Ahab.**

The Antichrist, one of the most tyrannical and evil men the Bible speaks about, will need to be trounced by a combination of these two strong anointings. Perhaps the Antichrist himself will combine the evil spirits that worked through both King Ahab and Pharaoh.

You will learn from this study, that God does specific things for specific reasons. You may want a miraculous ministry to impress people but God wants to fulfil His purpose. He may not want you to do any miracles. All He may want you to do, is to teach His Word. John the Baptist did not perform any miracles but he fulfilled his ministry. He prepared the way for Christ. Jesus said John the Baptist was the greatest prophet.

...Among them that are born of women there hath not risen a greater than John the Baptist...

Matthew 11:11

You can only line up with God's purpose. God will not do anything outside His purpose. When you fulfil God's purpose for your life, Jesus will call you "great". Find out the purpose of God and flow with it. It is the purpose of God that will be achieved at the end of the day, and not your purpose.

This is the purpose that is purposed upon the whole earth: and this is the hand that is stretched out upon all the nations.

For the Lord of hosts hath purposed, and who shall disannul it? and his hand is stretched out, and who shall turn it back?

Isaiah 14:26, 27

8. A new and original anointing

In this case, a person comes on the scene and God anoints him to do new things. This is not very common! A study of the Bible will show you that God rarely introduces a new and original anointing. The more common way by which God introduces anointing, is through people. Elijah the Tishbite is somebody who appeared with what I believe was a new and original anointing.

Two other people, Elisha and John the Baptist, have operated in the same anointing that was on Elijah. The difference was that, Elijah was walking in a *new and original anointing!* Elisha was walking in an *enhanced transferred anointing* and John the Baptist was walking in a *reintroduced anointing.*

CHAPTER 4

How to Understand the Anointing

It should be the desire of every real minister to catch the anointing. Without the anointing, your ministry is reduced to philosophy and your church to an ideological institution. If you want to have a big church, you need an anointing. If you want to teach the Word, you need an anointing. If you want to be a prophet you need to be anointed. Without the anointing, you are no nearer being a minister than I am to becoming the Prince of Wales.

There are a few important facts that people need to know about catching the anointing.

Five Important Facts about the Anointing

1. **It is difficult to get an anointing.**

   ...Elijah said unto Elisha, Ask what I shall do for thee, before I be taken away from thee. And Elisha said, I pray thee, let a double portion of thy spirit be upon me. And he said, Thou hast asked a hard thing...

   2 Kings 2:9, 10

Although this Scripture is usually referred to in terms of being anointed with a double portion, I believe that it also refers to the act of receiving an anointing. **It's a hard thing because few people have the anointing.** Many people try to get it, but few succeed. I can see why it is a hard thing.

Why is it that there are few doctors (relatively speaking) in the whole world? The answer is simple. It is because it is a "hard thing" to become a doctor. Many would like to be doctors, but few end up becoming doctors. In Ghana, like other countries, it is only the very best students who gain entry into the medical schools.

As I look around, I realize that there are not so many "truly" anointed ministers. Many may call themselves pastors, but few are really anointed to stand in that office. If they were anointed we would both know and see it. Though many have certificates and qualifications from Bible schools, few are actually anointed. This leads us to ask, "Why is it such a difficult thing to be anointed?"

2. You must have a strong desire for the anointing.

I want to show you why it is such a difficult thing for you to be anointed. **One reason why God does not readily give His anointing to just anyone is because the anointing is the Holy Spirit (God Himself).** The Holy Spirit is a precious gift from God to the Church. However, God does not haphazardly bestow that higher anointing needed for ministry on anyone. God does not cast His pearls before swine – you wouldn't!

If you don't value the anointing, God will not give it to you!

I once had an old car that I had used for a number of years. I wanted to give it to somebody. I searched earnestly for someone whom I could give it to. I knew that the car was very valuable and would cost millions of Ghanaian cedis (thousands of dollars) on the open market. However, because the car was slightly used I knew that if I gave it to the wrong person, he could mistakenly think I was getting rid of a worthless wreck. He would not appreciate it at all. Because of this, it took me a long time to decide whom to give it to.

There were many around me who desperately needed a car. But because I wasn't sure whether they would appreciate it or not, I decided to give it to a particular person. When I eventually gave the car away, I was happy with his response to the gift. I felt that he genuinely appreciated it. I am sure there were people who wondered why I didn't give the car to them.

God has a very precious commodity! He is looking for someone who really wants it and will appreciate it. Often, those who should be obvious recipients miss out on the blessing. The anointing then passes on to someone else, to the surprise of others.

Many wonder why God anointed someone like me. A visiting pastor once stood in my pulpit and overwhelmed by the huge crowds. He said, "The tables are turning. Many people are asking, *"Why Dag? Why is God using Dag?"* He was surprised that God had given me an anointing. Perhaps, in his estimation I shouldn't have received it.

Have you ever asked yourself why God loved Jacob and hated Esau?

3. Jacob desired the anointing.

As it is written, Jacob have I loved, but Esau have I hated.

Romans 9:13

Was Jacob not a heel snatcher and a deceiver? He was, but he desired the anointing. Often other earthly desires drown the desire for the anointing. You may be surprised that not meeting this qualification (of desiring the anointing) eliminates many people, as it did with my car gift.

Jacob strongly desired the birthright (anointing), but Esau did not care much about it. Something that should worry us is the fact that God hated Esau. If God hated Esau, then it is possible that God can hate you! If God hated Esau because he didn't care about the gift, then God can hate you because you don't care about the gift of His anointing. People have wondered why God used Kathryn Kuhlman, a healing evangelist. She married someone's husband and later on divorced him. I believe that she strongly desired the anointing.

4. God anoints the desirous.

God will pass over a thousand people who don't care much for the anointing and will give it to a person who strongly desires it. I see God passing over many people to get to you now!

Did you know that Elijah's first servant was not Elisha? Did you know that Elijah's first servant was bypassed when it was time to be anointed? This servant was active in ministry but he was not chosen to be anointed by God. It was this servant who Elijah sent seven times to see if the rain clouds had appeared.

...And Elijah went up to the top of Carmel; and he cast himself down upon the earth, and put his face between his knees, And said to his servant, Go up now, look toward the sea. And he went up, and looked, and said, There is nothing. And he said, Go again seven times.

1 Kings 18:42, 43

Why did this servant not receive the anointing? Why did Elisha, who was not even in the ministry, receive the anointing? Elisha was involved in business. He was plowing a field with his other business partners.

So he departed thence, and found Elisha the son of Shaphat, who was plowing with twelve yoke of oxen before him, and he with the twelfth...

1 Kings 19:19

What happened to the servant? Why wasn't he anointed? Why didn't he become the next great prophet? Please learn this important principle right now! God will pass over a thousand people who don't care much for the anointing and will give it to a person who strongly desires it.

Desire the anointing more than anything else in this world. That is the first step to becoming "anything" in the Kingdom of God. God told Pastor Timothy to look for people with a *desire* to be bishops. **It is people with strong desires who get spiritual gifts.**

Paul said,

Follow after charity, and desire spiritual gifts [anointing]...

1 Corinthians 14:1

If we could paraphrase this, it would say, "desire the anointing".

But covet [desire] earnestly the best gifts...

1 Corinthians 12:31

5. You can desire another minister's anointing.

I have learnt that you can specifically desire the anointing you see on a particular man of God. You can covet the gift that God has given to him. This is possible because Elisha specifically requested for the anointing that he saw on Elijah. Look around and see which man of God's ministry or gift you would like to have. I see that gift coming on you now!

Why would God tell you to desire something you cannot have? **The anointing is the principal tool for ministry. Without the anointing, all of your Bible school knowledge and certificates are useless.** You need an anointing. Anointing does not come by going to school. *Anointing is not taught, it is caught!*

When I was coming up in ministry, I did not know what I am teaching you now. God led me personally into this revelation. I loved the ministries of certain men and I followed hard after them.

The anointing that I unknowingly coveted began to operate in my life. I will share more about this later. God often uses a man or several different men to impact your life with the anointing.

When you have decided which gifts and anointing to covet, there are several hard steps or filters that you will have to go through. I call them filters because as people go through them, many "drop out". There are people who desire the anointing but never get it. It is because they are not able to pass through these tests. The steps are filters, which differentiate between the receivers and all others.

CHAPTER 5

Steps to the Anointing

7 Steps to the Anointing

1. The principle of vessel change

The anointing is like liquid that is poured into a vessel. Every liquid has a corresponding bottle or vessel. For instance, *Coca-Cola* will only be found in *Coca-Cola* bottles. *Sprite* has its own bottle. In order to be filled with Sprite you need to be a *Sprite* bottle. This is because specific fluids are associated with specific bottles. It is the same thing with the anointing.

Specific anointings are associated with certain types of people. An evangelistic anointing will go with a certain type of personality and character. A pastoral anointing will fit into a certain type of vessel. The Bible says that in a large house there are many types of vessels. You and I are those vessels.

But in a great house there are not only vessels of gold and of silver, but also of wood and of earth; and some to honour, and some to dishonour.

2 Timothy 2:20

If we want to be filled with a Coca-Cola anointing we need to be Coca-Cola bottles, so that the anointing will fit into us. If you study the Prophet Elijah, you will see a particular kind of anointing on his life. The prophetic anointing (1 Kings 18:36) on Elijah's life led him to do certain things. The anointing allows you to achieve certain things. He rebuked the kings of his day (1 Kings 21:17-20), fought with religious leaders (1 Kings 18:20-24), challenged sins and evil, was dramatic (1 Kings 18:30-39), and had his ministry ended by a woman, Jezebel (1 Kings 19:3,14,16).

The Bible tells us that John the Baptist operated in the same prophetic anointing as Elijah (Luke 1:76). We therefore see John the Baptist, rebuking the king of his day (Mark 6:17-20), confronting religious leaders (Matthew 3:7-10), fighting sin and evil and having a very dramatic ministry (Luke 3:7-14). We also see his ministry terminated by a woman, Herod's wife (Matthew 14:6-10). This was the anointing of Elijah at work.

Elijah's anointing operated in John's life because he was changed into a vessel that could receive it. Note that both John the Baptist (Mark 1:4) and Elijah (1 Kings 19:4) lived in the desert. Both Elijah and John the Baptist ate weird things – locusts (Matthew 3:4) and worms (1 Kings 17:6). Both John the Baptist (Matthew 3:4) and Elijah (2 Kings 1:8) wore clothes made of camel's hair.

To receive such a heavy prophetic healing anointing such as that on Elisha, a person cannot have problems such as lying, stealing and covetousness. The anointing of Elisha does not fit into lying and covetous vessels.

Unfortunately, Gehazi did not pass the test of lying and stealing. He lied and misrepresented Elisha! If a prophet is a liar, how will you know when he is speaking the Word of God? How would you know when he is speaking his own mind? Although Gehazi was close to the anointing, he did not obtain it! Elisha eventually cursed Gehazi for his unethical behaviour as a prophetic student.

The leprosy therefore of Naaman shall cleave unto thee, and unto thy seed for ever. And he went out from his presence a leper as white as snow.

2 Kings 5:27

If you desire a particular anointing, God will mould you into the type of vessel that can contain that anointing. If God wants you to be a great pastor, He may work on your education. He may work on your knowledge of administration and law. To receive the anointing you must allow Him to work on you!

Some people are not educated, nor do they educate themselves by reading. Yet, they desire the anointing to be leaders of large numbers of people. Don't you know that pastoring a large number of people means that you will have several highly educated people in your congregation? How will you relate with all of these people?

God may be working on your language. He may try to polish your manners and general etiquette! He may send you to a Bible school for training. He may send you off to a secular university for molding. I've had seven years of university training. Those years molded me into a suitable vessel. God may take you through various humbling experiences. All He is doing is preparing a vessel that can handle the anointing. This is the principle of vessel change.

If you desire a strong prophetic anointing, God is likely to require of you a life of solitude. You cannot have such an anointing if you do not make time to wait on the Lord.

You see, many changes may have to take place in your character and moral life if God is to use you for great achievements. **Those who refuse to change and to modify are refusing to be recipients of the anointing.**

This first step alone can explain why many people desire the anointing but never get it. Nobody pours *Coca-Cola* into a fuel tank. It is only petrol that is poured into a fuel tank. **If you are a fuel tank, you will never receive Coca-Cola – you will receive**

fuel! There are different containers for different anointings. Please accept this simple reality.

2. Servanthood

Throughout the Bible, those that received an anointing were servants. Joshua was a servant of Moses.

Now after the death of Moses the servant of the Lord it came to pass, that the Lord spake unto Joshua the son of Nun, Moses' minister, [servant]...

Joshua 1:1

Elisha was a servant of Elijah.

...Here is Elisha the son of Shaphat, which poured water [servant] on the hands of Elijah.

2 Kings 3:11

Peter, James and John were the servants of Christ.

HENCEFORTH I CALL YOU NOT SERVANTS [the disciples were ushers, bodyguards and errand boys]; for the servant knoweth not what his lord doeth: but I have called you friends...

John 15:15

The position of a servant is a humbling one. You do not have your own mind! You must work for your master, taking him to be right all the time. When you become a servant, you are like a grown up child, ready to receive every instruction that is meted out to you.

No one is above the Word of God. **If Joshua had to be a servant before he became an anointed General, so will you!** This is another reason why some people never become anointed. They are simply too big to ever become servants of anyone. They are too conscious of their age and position in society. They feel that their status must be constantly recognized. No wonder God has raised up many young people to receive an anointing. Many old dogs could not be taught new tricks.

Although God has given me several thousand people in my ministry, I have been a servant for many years. **I have served as an usher, drummer, arranger, sound technician and organist.** There is hardly any department of the church, in which I have not been a servant.

I marvel at those who want pastoral positions based on their having a Bible school diploma. They are no nearer to becoming pastors than I am to living on Mars. Some people just attend services and want to be appointed elders in the church, without serving their way to the top. These are the signs of a servant. Ask yourself if you are a servant or a boss.

13 Signs of a Servant

§   A servant has a master.

A son honoureth his father, and a servant his master...

Malachi 1:6

§   A servant is at the beck and call of his master.

For I am a man under authority, having soldiers under me: and I say to this man, Go, and he goeth; and to another, Come, and he cometh; and to my servant, Do this, and he doeth it.

Matthew 8:9

§   A servant is one who executes the command of another.

§   A servant cannot be inconvenienced by any job or task.

§   A servant does not see himself as equal to his master.

He doesn't say things like, "We are all classmates. We are all engineers. We all have children."

Who, being in the form of God, thought it not robbery to be equal with God:

Philippians 2:6

§ A servant carries out the wishes of his master.

Exhort servants to be obedient unto their own masters, and to please them well in all things; not answering again;

Titus 2:9

§ A servant cannot be embarrassed by his job.

And being found in fashion as a man, he humbled himself, and became obedient unto death, even the death of the cross.

Philippians 2:8

§ A servant does menial jobs: picking up crumbs, serving food..

When they were filled, he said unto his disciples, Gather up the fragments that remain, that nothing be lost.

John 6:12

...Elisha the son of Shaphat, which poured water on the hands of Elijah.

2 Kings 3:11

§ A servant promotes his master while he stays below.

He must increase, but I must decrease.

John 3:30

§ A servant does not expect thanks or acknowledgment.

So likewise ye, when ye shall have done all those things which are commanded you, say, We are unprofitable servants: we have done that which was our duty to do.

Luke 17:10

§   A servant does what his master wants in the way his master wants it.

…Behold, to obey is better than sacrifice, and to hearken than the fat of rams.

1 Samuel 15:22

§   A servant ministers to his master of his substance.

And certain women, which had been healed of evil spirits and infirmities, Mary called Magdalene, out of whom went seven devils.

And Joanna, the wife of Chuza Herod's steward, and Susanna, and many others, which ministered unto him of their substance.

Luke 8:2, 3

§   A servant has a reward.

Wherefore God also hath highly exalted him, and given him a name which is above every name:

Philippians 2:9

Looking unto Jesus the author and finisher of our faith; who for the joy that was set before him endured the cross, despising the shame, and is set down at the right hand of the throne of God.

Hebrews 12:2

3. Receiving a father

When God leads you to follow a man of God, (like Elisha followed Elijah) it is important for you to receive him as a father. You will notice from the story of Elisha that he had an earthly father called Shaphat.

...Here is Elisha the son of Shaphat...

2 Kings 3:11

However, by the time Elijah was taken away, Elisha referred to Elijah as his father. He did this effortlessly and naturally.

And Elisha saw it, and he cried, My father, my father...

2 Kings 2:12

Why is it important to receive your man of God as a father? What does it mean? I want to bring to your attention two very important reasons why you must receive him as a father.

Two Important Reasons for Receiving the Man of God as a Father

1. **Firstly, a person who does not have a father is very different from someone who has parents.**

A person with a father receives guidance and direction in life. A fatherless person has a life full of struggles.

I never worked whilst I was in university. My father provided for me fully until I became a doctor. The money he gave me each month as a student was even more than my salary when I became a doctor. My father bought me a brand new car when I was in the fifth year of medical school. I was really blessed to have a good father looking after me. **My life as a student was struggle free because I had a father!** However, the same cannot be said for many people.

I have met countless people who did not receive guidance in life. They threw away their talent and became non-entities in life, because there was no father to guide them. I know many people who do not even know their fathers.

The situation is worse for an orphan! Struggles abound for orphans. The future of an orphan is very uncertain. It is the same thing in ministry. When you have no one to influence you in the right way, your ministry is full of various struggles. Although I have had different fathers in ministry, there are times I have been fatherless as far as developing into a pastor was concerned.

I have had fathers in ministry from afar. I have gone through various struggles because I have not received support from nearby and potential fathers. Many of the struggles and frustrations I've experienced in ministry are because I had no one to help me in starting a church.

In fact, people who should have been fathers to me when I was beginning my church, were more of outright enemies. They opposed my cause and fought against me. Today, some of these people are always eager to claim fatherhood over my life because I am successful in ministry.

2. **The second reason why it is important to have a father is because inheritance flows naturally from a father to his children.**

In the ministry, spiritual inheritance flows naturally from the fathers to the sons. When my father died, his Will was read in court. He left his properties to his children. Although he had many employees and friends, he didn't leave anything to them – it all went to his children. Dear friend, that is the reality of life. Inheritance usually goes to children.

There is something known as a *spiritual inheritance* (Ephesians 1:18). **This spiritual inheritance of anointing and gifts passes naturally from fathers to sons.** It does not pass from father to equals, colleagues and friends. It does not even pass from father to servants. It passes from fathers to sons.

Hello Boss!

I used to have a junior pastor who preferred to call me "boss". I always felt uneasy when he called me "boss", but I didn't know why. You see, when someone calls you "boss", it means that he sees himself more as a hired hand. A few years later this pastor departed under unpleasant circumstances. Then I realized why I had felt uneasy.

A servant or an employee does not stay around forever. He's only there for awhile and will leave when it suits him.

And the servant abideth not in the house for ever: but the Son abideth ever.

John 8:35

So, if you have a relationship with a man of God which becomes a father-son relationship, then you can expect a spiritual inheritance of anointing to flow effortlessly from him to you.

How to Receive a Father

How do you receive someone as a father?

1. When someone is your father, he can speak freely into your life and you trust what he says.

A child usually believes that his father really cares for him, no matter how much the father disciplines him. If you have doubts in your mind about someone, or are suspicious of him, that person cannot be a father to you.

A pastor can be a good man of God to some people, but to others he becomes a father. When a person becomes a father to you, one of the main features is an attitude of fullest trust in him.

That attitude makes you admire and open up to him. You can never really open up your spirit to someone unless you trust him.

2. Maintain great respect and admiration for anyone you want to receive as a father.

Our father which art in heaven, hallowed be thy name (Matthew 6:9). Let the will of your father in ministry be done. If he tells you to pray and to fast, because you believe it is for your own good, allow that thing to happen.

3. Accept the father's position and authority.

Every time we pray the Lord's Prayer, we end it by saying, "thine is the kingdom, the power and the glory." We constantly affirm the position of our heavenly father. In the same way, every son must overcome the temptation to fight his father's authority and rule. **Never fight a father, it is a dangerous violation.** Instead, give the honour to the fathers.

The eye that mocketh at his father, and despiseth to obey his mother, the ravens of the valley shall pick it out, and the young eagles shall eat it.

Proverbs 30:17

4. Follow the man of God closely

Another important step is to follow the man of God closely. All the examples of people who received anointing, stayed close to their mentors. Elisha stayed with Elijah to the very end. Elijah tried on many occasions to get Elisha to stay behind, but he followed him to the very end. It was at the end that he caught the anointing. There are three ways you can follow a man of God closely.

3 Ways to Follow the Man of God

1. Physical association and close interaction

The first way is through physical association, close interaction and personal acquaintance with the anointed servant of God. Joshua associated with Moses as his personal servant and minister.

...Joshua the son of Nun, Moses' minister...

Joshua 1:1

Elisha desired a double portion of the anointing on Elijah's life. He knew that through service to the man of God he could obtain the anointing he desired.

Elisha became known as the person who physically washed the hands of Elijah. Close association of this sort may lead to a transfer of anointing.

...Here is Elisha the son of Shaphat, which poured water on the hands [cleaned and ministered] of Elijah.

2 Kings 3:11

2. Follow his words closely.

The second way by which you can follow a man of God is to follow his words closely. Not many people will have the privilege of interacting personally with their mentors. So how can anyone catch the anointing on a great man of God? The answer is simple. Is it the pouring of water or the doing of menial jobs that leads to a transfer of anointing? The answer is no! **The physical interaction exposes you to his words.**

Jesus said to His disciples, the words that I speak to you, they are Spirit (anointing) and life. **The anointing is in the words.** The disciples of Jesus soaked in the words of their master until He left them. **They took His words seriously because He had told them that the anointing was in the words.** Thank God that today the words of anointed ministers are available in books, tapes and videos.

...the words that I speak unto you, they are spirit [anointing], and they are life.

John 6:63

The anointing enters you as you listen to the Word. The Word is not just some philosophical discourse. It is different from a lecture in college. The Word is able to impart an anointing into your life. Look at this amazing Scripture in Ezekiel! The prophet said he could feel the anointing enter him as the Lord spoke to him.

And the spirit entered into me when he spake unto me...

Ezekiel 2:2

I have always wanted the opportunity to live and serve certain men of God. But that opportunity was never practical. However, following some of these men through videos, tapes and books has greatly blessed my life and ministry. The fact that you are reading this book is evidence that an anointing I received some years ago is real.

The Bible records that Elisha soaked in the words of his spiritual father. Elisha didn't just wash Elijah's hands. He didn't just wash and clean in the house. Just like Jesus and the disciples, Elisha and Elijah engaged in lots of important conversation.

And it came to pass, as they still went on, and talked...

2 Kings 2:11

3. Decide to stay close to the very end until the anointing which you desire is flowing through your ministry.

Elisha walked so closely to Elijah that God had to separate them Himself. Don't allow anyone to separate you from your spiritual father. Do not allow circumstances to keep you away from your man of God.

...there appeared a chariot of fire, and horses of fire, and parted them both asunder...

2 Kings 2:11

5. Spiritual ministrations

We must be careful not to make any mistakes. God will give you the anointing. No man can give you the anointing. Yet, He does it through men. It is important to pray and ask for the anointing.

If ye then, being evil, know how to give good gifts unto your children: how much more shall your heavenly Father give the Holy Spirit to them that ask him?

Luke 11:13

Another way you can receive the anointing is through the *laying on of hands*. The laying on of hands is a foundational doctrine of the Church. It is the principal way in which an impartation or gift is given. It is such an important procedure that God tells us not to hurriedly impart gifts through the laying on of hands.

Lay hands suddenly on no man, neither be partaker of other men's sins: keep thyself pure.

1 Timothy 5:22

Timothy, the pastor, had hands laid on him and he received spiritual gifts. The Bible plainly declares that he received the gift of God through the laying on of hands.

Wherefore I put thee in remembrance that thou stir up the gift of God, which is in thee by the putting on of my hands.

2 Timothy 1:6

This means that the manifestation of the gift and anointing must have begun to operate in Timothy's life after hands were laid on him. Thank God for the preaching of the Word of God. There is a place for the laying on of hands. The disciples received an anointing when Jesus breathed on them and said,

…Receive ye the Holy Ghost:

John 20:22

These different spiritual ministrations are ways by which God can impart His gift to you.

6. The passage of time

Time is a very important element in the development of any ministry. The Word of God teaches us that Jesus adds to our gifts when He recognizes that we are faithful to what He has given to us.

He that is faithful in that which is least is faithful also in much: and he that is unjust in the least is unjust also in much.

Luke 16:10

With the passage of time your faithfulness will be tested. Your faithfulness will provoke God to give you additional gifts and a greater anointing. You will discover that certain realms are inaccessible to you until "time" elapses. Unfortunately, there is no substitute for the test of time.

Some years ago, I tried to raise the dead but I did not succeed. I often wondered why God did not honour me then. If He had, I probably would have backslidden by now. I now see certain things happening in my ministry, which I didn't see before. If I had had that level of anointing some years ago, it could have destroyed me. It is important to trust God to allow time to pass so that He Himself can lift you up at the right time.

7. Minister to the man of God

The last but not the least step I want to share with you is about ministering to the man of God with your substance.

And certain women, which had been healed of evil spirits and infirmities, Mary called Magdalene, out of whom went seven devils, And Joanna, the wife of Chuza Herod's steward, and Susanna, and many others, which ministered unto him of their substance.

Luke 8:2, 3

You must be able to minister to the man of God out of your own substance. If money is a problem to you then you cannot be a minister. The Bible teaches that people who have been taught should share their good things with those who teach them.

Let him that is taught in the word communicate unto him that teacheth in all good things.

Galatians 6:6

The man of God will minister spiritual things to you and you will minister back to him in physical things. The anointing is provoked when you minister to the man of God. Anytime I have had the opportunity to be near those who have been a blessing to me, I have ministered to them out of my substance.

When the woman with the alabaster box of ointment ministered to Christ, He said that she would be remembered. When you pour an "alabaster box" on a man of God you will provoke a blessing and be remembered. **Your ministry will have a longer life span as you decide to honour those before you. Your ministry will be remembered by many.** You will provoke the favour and anointing of God over your life.

Notice what great men like Abraham did when they met with greater men of God. They immediately ministered to the man of God out of their substance.

And Melchizedek king of Salem brought forth bread and wine: and he was the priest of the most high God. And he blessed him,... And he [Abraham] gave him tithes of all.

Genesis 14:18-20

CHAPTER 6

What it Means to Catch the Spirit of the Ministry

Your aspiration for church growth will naturally lead you to work with many different people. It is only understandable that in a larger ministry you will need more "hands on deck". The act of recruiting new people often leads to the destruction of the ministry. Be careful that you do not end up destroying what you are trying to build. It is important to recruit people who have what I call the spirit of the ministry.

> **And I will come down and talk with thee there: and I will take of the spirit which is upon thee, and will put it upon them; and they shall bear the burden of the people with thee, that thou bear it not thyself alone.**
>
> **Numbers 11:17**

Please notice the revelation that God gave Moses. He said, "I'm going to take of the spirit or anointing that is upon you and that same anointing will be transferred to other people." It is only then that they will be able to work with you. It is only then that they will be able to help you.

God could have simply given these seventy people an anointing for leadership, but He didn't. **God did not give them a general anointing for leadership! Neither did He give them a special anointing of management and wise judgement! He simply gave them Moses' anointing.** What was the spirit upon Moses? It was the special gift of ministry given to Moses to lead the people. This is what those seventy pastors received.

There is an anointing on every ministry. That is why people can start out in a ministry of their own and have only twenty people after ten years. Were these people to operate under a certain ministry, they would not have only twenty people after ten years. They may have a thousand. This is because different ministries have different anointings over them.

I am not saying that you do not have to start something new, not at all! I am saying that God gives certain gifts to certain men. Those who find themselves planted under such men find that they are catching the same spirit of ministry. They will find themselves doing great things or even greater things than he is doing.

There Is a Difference!

Catching the spirit of the ministry is a little different from catching the anointing. When you join a new church, you will notice that it is different from any other church. **Understand that every church is different and has its own culture.** Every minister has a peculiar anointing on his life. This leads to a unique ministry. When you join up with this unique ministry, you must adapt and flow with it. Understand that every church is different. When you join a church, you have to acclimatize and re-learn certain things. It is the senior pastor's duty to prevent anyone from becoming a minister without adapting fully to the culture of the church.

It is the trainee's duty to learn, imbibe, observe and adapt to the spoken and unspoken philosophies of the church. Study the culture. Flow with it. Do all you can to fit in. When you fit in, that peculiar anointing will also fit into you and operate through you. It is possible and it is necessary if you want to be fruitful in the context of a particular church.

If you do not adapt, the anointing will not be able to fit into you because it was meant for a particular type of vessel. You will run into problems if you choose to ignore the standards accepted and used by the general leadership. **When people do not operate under the same Spirit (anointing), they create conflict.** The leaders become disunited and each one thinks he is right. The church begins to disintegrate behind the scenes and soon this comes into the open.

How to Catch the Spirit of the Ministry

To catch the spirit of the ministry, you have to company with the church and its leadership. There is simply no other way. You have to know what they do, and watch them do it! You have to accept it in your mind and believe in it in your heart. The standards and principles in the church must become yours. They must no longer be "their" principles.

When you think like the leadership, you have caught the spirit of the ministry.

The anointing makes you think in a particular way. The anointing makes you act in a particular way.

I learnt long ago that I should not accept people who do not really fit in as sons, into my ministry. Someone may be a well-qualified minister with great credentials, but if he does not have the spirit of the ministry, it is no use taking him on. The few conflicts that I have experienced in the Lighthouse denomination have been through and from people who did not fully catch the spirit of this ministry. It looked as though they fitted in, but in reality, they were not a part of us.

After Jesus ascended into Heaven, a replacement was sought for Judas. They chose someone who had the spirit of Jesus' ministry. Someone who knew them through and through. They needed someone who had accepted the standards and philosophies of Christ. They did not want to introduce somebody who would create confusion within their ranks.

> **Wherefore of these men which have companied with us all the time that the Lord Jesus went in and out among us, Beginning from the baptism of John, unto that same day that he was taken up from us, must one be ordained to be a witness with us...**

> **Acts 1:21, 22**

You will observe in the above Scripture that they chose somebody who had been with them long enough to catch the spirit of the ministry. They didn't care whether the person had the gift of prophecy or the gift of leadership. It is better to be safe than sorry. Go for those you know and avoid unknown elements!

There are three groups of people I do not often consider for employment. These are not "bad" people! They are good people but they need to catch the spirit of the ministry.

Three Groups of People I Will Not Employ

a. A Bible school graduate seeking employment in the church

Graduating from a Bible school means very little to me. All it means is that you have a piece of paper showing that you have studied some courses. Those courses may be different from the courses I teach in my church. Even if they are the same, they may have a completely different orientation.

I ask such people to simply join the church and become a part of the church family. They must then go through the ranks like every other church member. *If and only if he is able to catch the spirit of the ministry, can he be part of its leadership.*

b. An experienced and seasoned minister

There is a saying, "You can't teach an old dog new tricks". This saying is not in the Bible but it is often true. When a tree is young, you can bend it. But when a tree is old, you must break it in order to get it to bend! Usually, people who have been in the ministry for years feel that they know all about the ministry. Such people have problems fitting in. After being a part of your system for a while, they will say, "I was a pastor before I joined you", "I was a minister in my own right before I came here." They will add, "I had a ministry before I came here and I just decided to place it under your ministry." **Such people do not fit in because they are not prepared to be trained or retrained.**

I have learnt from painful experience to train up my own sons and daughters in ministry. They are to me, like the disciples were to Jesus. I can trust them and I can leave my ministry in their hands wherever they are in the world. Jesus left His ministry to twelve men and they handled it perfectly. When you have people who have caught the spirit of the leadership you can leave things with them and not worry. They will not rebel.

c. A pastor of a small church who wants to join a larger network

This is even more dangerous! When the church begins to grow under a new name and new anointing, the pastor will begin to have thoughts of breaking away. He will say, "I had a church with members before I joined up with you. I want to change the name back to what it was before." This often leads to painful splits and breakaways. At this point, no one will know who is really right or wrong.

My policy is to encourage such individuals to continue independently in ministry.

If he insists, the way forward is for him to close down his church and join the bigger network as an ordinary member. With the process of time, such a person may become a minister within the network and start a church again. However, it takes a lot of humility to do something like that.

It is important for senior pastors to know when people have caught the spirit of the ministry. It is important for up-and-coming ministers to understand how to catch the spirit of the ministry.

Eight Things You Must Catch

In every church, you must endeavour to catch the *vision, principles, philosophy, standards, doctrines, procedures, emphasis* and the *anointing* of the house. To illustrate this better I will just use Lighthouse Chapel International as a model.

1. The vision of the house

Generally speaking, the vision of Lighthouse Chapel International is soul winning and church planting. Many pastors do not have a vision for soul winning. We have a strong vision for soul winning. If you are not oriented towards the harvest, you will be a misfit in such a church.

Everyone is taught and motivated to save the lost and to be involved in practical ministry. No one is left out, including professionals and businessmen. **We believe that every member can be a minister.** It may sound strange, but that is our vision.

Some churches have a vision for prosperity. Others have a vision for dominion over the works of darkness. Others have a vision for deliverance. Whichever church you decide to be a part of, you must learn to catch the vision of that house. No one vision is right or wrong. The vision depends on the call that God has given to the man. Leave the judgement of that to the Lord.

2. The principles of the house

The principles of LCI are the principles in the Word of God. One of our principles is that everything must be founded on the solid foundation of the Bible. It is our principle to reject things that are not firmly based on the Word of God.

We have principles of loyalty. People who break these principles cannot fit into our ministry. I am loyal to my pastors and I expect them to be loyal to me. We believe in principled leadership where everyone can climb to the highest position in ministry.

3. The philosophy of the house

The philosophy of the house refers to the general trend of thinking. Our church believes that lay people must do the work of ministry. We believe that the educated can also be in ministry.

We believe that church buildings are very important for the establishment of the church. We believe that church buildings bring stability and permanence. Church building projects allow church members to know that their money is being "put to good use". We also believe in frugality. There are many ways by which we save money. Ironically, this makes people think that we are rich.

Another important philosophy of LCI is that we are pro-marriage. We encourage people to marry, and to do so at a young age. We feel that it is the biblical pattern for young people to marry and stay pure, rather than to live in sin and hypocrisy. Any leader within our system must have these ideas as *his own* ideas.

4. The standards of the house

In our church, we expect people to be faithful to their marriage partners. We expect ministers to lead honest lives and to have financial and moral integrity. We do not compromise on these standards! We do not expect people to be perfect, but we do expect them to be honest.

A lowering of the standards of any church will lead to a gradual and complete deviation from the original vision of the church. It is because of the lowering of standards that gay and lesbian priests and even bishops are now a part of church life. Some priests are officiating the marriages between two men. They are thereby claiming God's approval on homosexuality. This is Sodom and Gomorrah coming into the church. How did it get there? It got there by gradually changing the standards of the Church of God.

5. The doctrines of the house

Within every church there are certain beliefs based on the Bible. A doctrine is a trend of teaching. One of our doctrines is the doctrine of loyalty.

We teach extensively on this. *(For further study see my book Loyalty & Disloyalty).*

Another doctrine we have is what we call, Anagkazo. This Greek word means something to every leader in our church. It teaches about compelling souls to come to Christ. You cannot be a minister in our church if you do not understand and believe in Anagkazo.

6. The procedures of the house

The way things are done in every church is different. In our church, a person becomes a pastor by rising through the ranks.

One must first be a shepherd before being promoted to a lay pastor. That is just the way things are done here. We have very few full-time ministers.

We believe that you must first be successful as a lay pastor before becoming a full-time minister. This may be different from the way you do things in your church, but if you want to be in a particular ministry, you must accept the procedures of that house.

You cannot be a leader in the church if you do not pay tithes, or what we call First and Best Fruits. That is just the way we do things. Every Lighthouse church takes two offerings on Sundays. In our church, you must have extensive counselling before getting married. These are just some of the procedures we do not intend to alter. Anyone who is going to be a leader of the church has to accept these procedures and flow with them.

The church has a system of small groups involving fellowships, ministries and chapels. This system has worked for us throughout the world, wherever Lighthouse churches have been established.

That is the way we do things. That is our procedure. Welcome to the house.

7. The emphasis of the house

Every ministry has a peculiar emphasis. We emphasize the preaching and the teaching of the Word of God.

Some emphasize prosperity and healing. Some emphasize the anointing. We emphasize the winning of souls and the establishing of the church. Mind you, we believe in miracles, and we experience great moves of the Spirit, but our emphasis is the Word. If you accept this emphasis then you can be with us.

8. The anointing of the house

This is the anointing that we have been talking about in the earlier chapters. Apart from getting the natural and physical aspects like the procedures and standards, you need to get this spiritual component.

There is nothing like the anointing. Without it, you can do nothing in ministry. Once you have tasted the anointing and the difference it makes to ministry, you will not like to do anything without it. If you are within a particular church, the principal anointing that you should desire is the anointing on your leader. This is because you are working under his ministry.

CHAPTER 7

How to Start a Church

Many people are afraid of starting a church because they do not know how to pioneer a new work. **The art of beginning a church is the art of witnessing, following-up and gathering sheep together.** You do not need to break up someone's church to begin your own! How would you feel if someone was building his house next to yours and decided to break down your house to get some blocks for his? That is madness!

Unfortunately, this seems to be the only way that some people feel they can start a church. From today, do not be afraid of starting out in an honourable way. If God has really spoken to you, it will succeed!

Ten Steps You Need to Start a Church

1. **Count the cost.**

   For which of you, intending to build a tower, sitteth not down first, and counteth the cost...

   Luke 14:28

Carefully consider the implications of starting a church. It is not going to be easy! Not many people want to identify with a small thing. I learnt many years ago that there are two types of people in the world. There are those who push the canoe from the sand into the sea. Then there are those who jump into it when it is safely on the water.

When the canoe is on the sand, it is very difficult to push into the water. When it is on the water it is safer and many more people jump in. That is why it is easier for a large church to grow.

When I began in the ministry, I was despised and opposed! Looking back, I am surprised that I was able to survive the storms of beginning a church on my own. At certain times, I felt like giving up. Everyone in the world seemed against me. They called me names and ridiculed me.

When I carried a set of drums from my room in the medical school hostel to a nearby classroom, I must have looked like a crazy zealot! They were thinking,"What does this person think he is doing with a few medical and nursing students?"

I had no help from any of the bigger churches of my day. Some of them ridiculed me whilst others even opposed me. There was no help or approval from any man of God.

2. Do not become desperate.

Do not become financially desperate in the early stages of ministry. Be careful not to become dependent on the church you are pioneering for your financial survival.

That is a big mistake! If you do, you will become a desperate man, clutching at every straw for survival.

A small church usually cannot afford to pay the salary of a pastor, much less buy him a car. **My advice to anyone who is beginning a church is to find a job and start the church as a lay person.** When people see that you are not ministering for financial gain, they will be more interested in your new church.

Too many pastors are desperate for more and more offerings from their few members. Sixteen people cannot look after you. Twenty-one people cannot support your upkeep and your children's school fees.

Don't be a desperate pastor! Get a job right now! At the right time, the church will have more than enough money to look after its pastors.

I had to invest a lot of my own money to get the church to work. Although I am now in full-time ministry, I was not paid for the first five years of the church's existence. There is another reason why you should not draw a salary in the early stages of a church. Money will be needed to buy equipment and pay other expenses like rent. If you siphon out the lifeblood of the church, it will not develop normally.

3. Two or three is enough.

How many people are needed to start a church? The answer is in the Bible! Two or three!

For where two or three are gathered together in my name, there am I in the midst of them.

Matthew 18:20

Some people have criticized me for having two or three people in a church. Well, such criticism comes from an ignoramus. I would rather hear my dogs barking in the morning than to listen to critical and inexperienced scoffers!

I do not start my churches with half a section of another person's church. If I have one pastor who is ready to obey God, all I need to do is to send him and he will start the work. The Lighthouse Cathedral was started with as few as five people.

When I went to Zürich in Switzerland to start a church, I knew only one person. Today that church has several hundred people in it. One pastor who did not know anybody in South Africa, but was willing to do the work of God, started our church in

South Africa. **You do not need more than one person to start a church.** I have churches that have only three people, and I am not ashamed to say it. Do not try to impress anyone, just do the work of God!

Sometimes people are afraid to pioneer a church because they do not know how to do basic Christian tasks. What do I mean by the basics? The basics are praying, witnessing and following up converts.

If you are truly called of God, then the only person you need is yourself! All churches which began in this way have grown to become great trees. The Bible says that the Kingdom of God is like a mustard seed.

...The kingdom of heaven is like to a grain of mustard seed, which a man took, and sowed in his field: Which indeed is the least of all seeds: but when it is grown, it is the greatest among herbs, and becometh a tree, so that the birds of the air come and lodge in the branches thereof.

Matthew 13:31, 32

What does that mean? Whereas an Old Boys' Association or a Keep Fit Club may begin with quite a number of people, the beginnings of a church are like insignificant seeds. They can grow, and they will grow. Many of my pastors are surprised when their churches grow. They cannot believe that the church will work. The beginning looks so miserable yet that is how the Kingdom of God is.

The Megachurch Had One Member!

One day, one of my pastors went to church and only one person came. He told me that he was very discouraged and depressed. He led that one person in worship. Then he preached to that one person. Afterwards he took an offering from that one person and then closed the service. He narrated to me how he went back home to his apartment in the deepest and blackest depression of his life. I am happy to tell you that today his church is a megachurch and is growing.

4. Don't be in a hurry.

There isn't any tree that grows from a seed into a large tree overnight. No human being grows to be six feet tall in one year. No two-year old grows into an eighteen-year old within six months. *If you have a hasty spirit, you will not be successful at starting a church.*

He that hasteth to be rich hath an evil eye, and considereth not that poverty shall come upon him.

Proverbs 28:22

In fact, when you are in a hurry, you are likely to cut corners, break someone's church and criticize those ahead of you. You will commit dangerous sins in the early days of your fledgling ministry.

Do not expect much within a year. Don't be surprised if you only have twenty people after two years. The mustard seed will surely grow into a megachurch!

5. Pray for and recruit pillars.

Pray for labourers. Ask God to give you helpers. Then go out and recruit pillars. Jesus called individuals to follow Him. Jesus recruited Simon and Andrew. Then He also recruited James and John.

Now as he walked by the sea of Galilee, he saw Simon and Andrew his brother... And Jesus said unto them, Come ye after me, and I will make you to become fishers of men.

Mark 1:16, 17

And when he had gone a little farther thence, he saw James the son of Zebedee, and John his brother...

And straightway he called them... and they left their father... and went after him.

Mark 1:19, 20

These people later became pillars in the church.

And when James, Cephas, and John, who seemed to be pillars...

Galatians 2:9

Sometimes you need to travel far in order to convince certain important pillars to join your church. **Be extra careful that you do not break down somebody's church in the process of building your own.**

Making an open invitation to all is different from coercing people to leave their church to join you. The very existence of a church is an open invitation. Remember that you will reap what you sow (Galatians 6:7). If you pressurize pillars in another person's church to leave, it will happen to you one day.

One important aspect in recruiting people is to pray for labourers. Let it be your daily prayer topic. Ask God for workers and committed people. Pray for people who will be loyal to you in everything that you do. Pray for people who will support you.

Pray ye therefore the Lord of the harvest, that he will send forth labourers into his harvest.

Matthew 9:38

6. Lay a foundation of prayer.

I recommend an average time of prayer and fasting of three weeks or more. Pray for the future of the church. Do not expect results next week. The answer to these prayers will be seen in the years ahead.

When I first came to Korle-Bu (the area in Accra where our church is located), every night at ten o'clock,I would go to the beach to pray together with four other medical students. We would pray up until midnight. As I stood on the rocks near the seashore, my prayer was simply, "Lord, let your will be done. Do whatever you want to do with my life." As the years have gone by, the Lord has answered this prayer beyond my wildest imagination.

I believe in laying a solid foundation of prayer and fasting at the beginning of every church. The church is a spiritual entity and not a social club. It must be established on scriptural and spiritual foundations.

Some useful Scriptures in praying for church establishment and church growth are:

...Thy will be done...

Matthew 6:10

Thy kingdom come...

Matthew 6:10

Ask of me, and I shall give thee the heathen for thine inheritance,...

Psalm 2:8

...enlarge my coast...

1 Chronicles 4:10

...increase them with men like a flock.

Ezekiel 36:37

...for as soon as Zion travailed, she brought forth her children.

Isaiah 66:8

...I travail in birth again...

Galatians 4:19

7. Be a motivational leader.

After gathering a few people into a room, you will need to greatly encourage them, including yourself. People will be thinking in their minds, "Are you out of your mind? Is this what you call a church?" You must learn to do what David did when faced with discouragement – *Encourage yourself first.*

...but David encouraged himself in the Lord his God.

1 Samuel 30:6

Then you must encourage the people. Tell them that though the beginning seems to be small, the future is going to be great!

Though thy beginning was small, yet thy latter end should greatly increase.

Job 8:7

Tell them not to despise the small start. Explain to them that the end is always better than the beginning. When they see that you are encouraged, they will be motivated to continue with the church.

Better is the end of a thing than the beginning thereof...

Ecclesiastes 7:8

For who hath despised the day of small things?

Zechariah 4:10

Tell them that they are privileged to be founding members of a great church. Explain that the foundation of a building is the most important part of a building. Therefore, they are the most important members that the church will ever have. Tell them that Jesus always had a special place and reward for the apostles because they were His foundational members.

And are built upon the foundations of the apostles...

Ephesians 2:20

81

Do not make the mistake of rebuking and shouting at them. Do not vent your frustration on your few members. It is not their fault that the church is small in the beginning stages. Preach faith! Preach hope! Preach stabilization! Preach about a better tomorrow! People love to hear that tomorrow will be better than today. You must be bold and shameless in your preaching.

I say unto you, Though he will not rise and give him, because he is his friend, yet because of his importunity [shamelessness] he will rise and give him as many as he needeth.

Luke 11:8

In the above passage, the Greek word Anaideia translated importunity also means *shamelessness*. The shamelessly persistent person gets results. Let's face it! There is some amount of shame in beginning a ministry with a few people. That is why people despise small beginnings!

Shamelessness (Anaideia) must characterize all that you do when you begin a church. Shamelessly invite people to join you on Sunday morning. When they see that you are not shy of your church, they will be interested in coming. Shamelessly advertise your church.

People will believe what you say about your church. If you have an assistant, he must say good things about the preaching and about the church in general. All of these things help to create a good atmosphere for church growth.

8. Witnessing and follow-up.

This must be predominant in all your church activities. You must boldly enter into the houses of your city and preach Christ to the people. You must shamelessly lead people to Christ in their living rooms. Pray for them and invite them to church.

Stand on the street and talk to passers-by about Jesus Christ. If you cannot shamelessly do street evangelism, then you cannot be a pastor. Lead the congregation in inviting people to church every Sunday. Do not be depressed if most of the visitors do not come back. Most of them will not stay anyway. God will supernaturally bring the increase.

Pastors must realize that there is a spiritual principle of sowing and reaping. Whatever you sow, you will reap.

...for whatsoever a man soweth, that shall he also reap.

Galatians 6:7

If you sow seeds through invitations and witnessing, you will reap from it one day. My experience is that after a crusade or an outreach, we initially have very few results. However, after a while, we begin to have people coming from the very place we did the outreach to church. Usually they are not the people we witnessed to, but God divinely sends them to us from that place. Use all the principles of *'anagkazo'* (For further study, see my book 'Anagkazo').

9. Avoid these mistakes.

Do not hurriedly appoint people to leadership positions. Allow time to pass before you make definite appointments. Many of the people who are with you in the beginning will leave anyway. **Do not be discouraged because of fluctuating attendance.** Do not be discouraged because of a rotational shift of the members, i.e., half attend this week, the other half next week. *That is how sheep behave. Take no notice of them!*

Do not rent an expensive hall. Do not keep the church's money in your house or in your personal account. One day somebody will accuse you of stealing, although you may have contributed a lot to the church. Do not count the money yourself, but assign people to do so.

10. You don't need these things.

Contrary to what people think, several things are not necessary when you are starting a church. *You do not need a complimentary card or a briefcase to build a mega church! A constitution is not vital in the early stages.* What is important is to have members and a regular congregation. A church logo is not important, neither is a church flag.

Initially, it may not be necessary to register a church. Many countries allow freedom of association and freedom of religion. Just build the church and fill it with people. Pray for them, preach the Word, visit the sheep and trust God! Since the Greater One is in you, you cannot fail!

CHAPTER 8

Fight for Commitment

If you want your church to grow you must fight to have more committed members. Committed members are the building blocks of a large church. **The key to increasing in size is to have more and more very committed people.**

Let's consider for example if you are in a situation where you are building a house. Supposing you laid a hundred blocks on your building foundation everyday. At the end of the day you might look at the work done and say to yourself, "Things are getting better. The building is coming up nicely!"

How would you feel if you noticed that seventy of those blocks were missing every morning? You would feel very frustrated because your building project would progress at a much slower rate. The building would still develop, however at a much slower rate. This is because of the regular loss of the building blocks. In the case of a church, the building blocks are the members. The missing blocks are the uncommitted members who disappear ever so often.

In order to develop committed members, every pastor must know about the different levels of commitment each member may have. Do not be deceived by a large crowd. **A large** crowd consists of people with different levels of commitment. **You must press for the highest level of commitment possible from every one of your members.** Over the years, I have observed four main types of commitment.

Four Main Types of Commitment

1. Fair weather commitment

The lowest type of commitment is Fair Weather Commitment. This consists of those who are committed when things are going well. The Bible says a rich man has many friends, but a poor man does not have many friends.

Wealth maketh many friends; but the poor is separated from his neighbour.

Proverbs 19:4

When I started out in ministry, I had few friends. When the ministry became large and successful, many people claimed to be my friends. Many spoke of imaginary assistance they gave me in my early days. Senior ministers have sworn that they never said negative things about me (although I know they did). When things are not going well, people don't want to know you. But when the sky is clear, they all claim to be your friends.

Fair weather church members are people who are committed only when things are going well. They form the crowds that come when the church is flourishing and successful. Such people fall away when a crisis or problem arises. You cannot rely on such people when building a Megachurch. People with fair weather commitment are usually not aware of their low level of commitment. Therefore, the pastor must preach and teach against being committed only when things are going well.

2. Situational friendship commitment

The next type of commitment is what I call situational *friendship commitment.* Friends are committed to each other to some extent. There are also two levels of commitment between friends, *situational friendship commitment and non-situational friendship commitment.*

There are two types of friends in the world. There are friends, who are friends because the *situation* permits. In school, for instance, different situations bring people together and make them friends. Everyone has friends like that. You had to sit in the same classroom for some years and you became friends because of the circumstances. However, when you left school or didn't see these friends anymore, you stopped relating with them. I have many friends like that.

Some people are only committed to their church when the situation permits. They may live near the church or there may be no other church nearby. However, if another church were to start in the vicinity they would go there. You may have many people in your church, but they are only members because of their circumstances. Such people cannot be relied upon. You must press for a higher commitment.

Aim to get all of your members to be committed irrespective of their circumstances. That is *non-situational commitment.* They are committed to you irrespective of the situation. Some children come to the church because their parents do so, however, if their parents were not to come anymore they would stop coming to church.

Attack Sunday

Our church was once attacked by traditional practitioners. On that Sunday morning an armed mob of people invaded the church, threw rocks at the church and physically assaulted several of our church members and pastors. I believe they were hunting for me on that fateful morning. The attack so startled us that it has been ingrained in our memories. After the attack, we had to wash away streams of blood from the church grounds.

Many of our church members were hurt and the entire incident was broadcast on national television. As you would expect, this caused the *"fair weather"* and *"situational friendship"* members to vanish for several weeks. Someone whose commitment is deep, will not be moved by such attacks.

On that Sunday, many cars were vandalized, with their windscreens smashed. However, the next Sunday, the committed members were back in church with their cars. They were members, whether they were attacked or not. In fact, some have expressed their commitment to die for the church if there is any further attack.

Members whose commitment is at the level of *"fair weather"* and *"situational friendship"* are not of much use to the church in times of crisis. The pastor must preach to raise the level of commitment of all members.

3. Non-situational friendship commitment

When your church members have graduated to this level of commitment, they are not moved by hurts, separation, conflicts or distance. You can rely more on such people.   The commitment is one of deep friendship. It is not affected much by circumstances. Pastors should aim at moving their members to at least this level.

I have friends I don't see often.   For instance, one of my university roommates, "Dr. Nosh", is a non-situational friend. That means he's my friend whether I see him or not. We live in different parts of the world, yet our friendship is not affected by distance or separation. I know he's my friend and he knows I am his friend. He can depend on me and I can depend on him. Like Jonathan and David, their friendship became a bond between them.

> **And Jonathan caused David to swear again, because he loved him: for he loved him as he loved his own soul.**
>
> **1 Samuel 20:17**

4. Marital commitment

There is an even higher level of commitment – *marital commitment.* In marital commitment, the individuals are committed as though they are married. In marriage, there should be no thought of divorce, but rather a spirit of permanence. There are no more options left.

You cannot decide to stay or leave. You must stay; it is as simple as that! You are in it for good. There may be conflicts, challenges and even disappointments, but this will have no ability to shake the commitment of a married couple.

Like everyone else, I have had challenges in my marriage. I have had happy times and not so happy times. Nevertheless, I never consider the option of divorce. That option has been ruled out by the Word of God and by my level of commitment. Nothing can and nothing should be able to separate a married couple. **Our commitment to Christ is at the marital level of commitment.** The Bible teaches that we are supposed to be married to Christ.

> **Wherefore my brethren…that ye should be married to another, even to him who is raised from the dead, that we should bring forth fruit unto God.**
>
> **Romans 7:4**

When the commitment to the church rises to the level of marital commitment, the Bible teaches that we will begin to bring forth fruit unto God. The higher the commitment, the more the fruit. **It is only when a man and woman have marital commitment that they can successfully bring forth fruit (children).**

This is the type of commitment I expect from all pastors, leaders and mature members in the church. I am committed to them for life and I expect them to be committed to me for life. When a church has a pastor who is unstable, the congregation can feel the instability. The church members are not ready to give their best if they feel that the pastor is there for just a season.

The Temporary Associate

One day I was visited in my office by a senior pastor and his associate. I asked him,

"How is the ministry?"

"We're not doing badly," he said. "We are having a few struggles though."

They continued, "As you know, our church has been going through one crisis after another."

The senior pastor continued, "It has not been easy. One person after the other keeps leaving the church."

Out of curiosity, I asked the associate, "Do you have any plans of starting your own ministry one day?"

"Certainly!" he said. "I am just working with this man for a while, then I will launch out on my own."

"Oh, I see."

I told him (in front of his associate), "If I were you, I would not like to work with someone who is using me as a springboard to start his own ministry."

I warned him, "When this pastor eventually leaves you, it will cause a lot of pain and conflict in the church."

"Really!" he exclaimed.

I advised him, "I personally do not believe that your closest associate should have such a low level of commitment. I think a pastor in the church should have the highest level of commitment. I believe he should have what I call marital commitment."

"I only want to work with people who are committed. This is because I can then pour out my life into them."

I explained further, "Take a young man and a young lady who are courting each other. A decent young woman would not be prepared to undress and perform acts of great commitment with her fiancé. However, if this young man takes his fiancée to the marriage altar and signs a legal contract, then he can expect the highest level of commitment (till death us do part) from her. That same decent young lady would then be prepared to give her utmost commitment and flow into the deepest level of involvement."

"Do you understand what I am saying," I said to this pastor.

He seemed to understand what I was saying.

"I would not like to get deeply involved with people unless they guarantee me the highest level of commitment," I added.

Not long after, this senior pastor called me saying, "Just as you predicted, my associate has left me suddenly and it has caused me a lot of pain."

At the time I had the conversation with him, he had about seventy members in his church. However, after the associate left the church, he was left with only twenty people. The lack of a high level of commitment from associates and pastors is very damaging to a church. *The congregation follows what they see the pastors do.* If they see shallow commitment, they in turn will have a low level of commitment.

Let's be committed to one another. I am the type of person who gives my utmost to help people. I do not want to pour out my life and soul into people only for them to despise and destroy me.

Preach marital commitment. Teach marital commitment. The commitment of your members will rise. They will become solid building blocks of your mega church. Anytime you speak to a church member, assess his or her level of commitment. Try to place him in one of these four levels. Then you must work on him or her for a higher level of commitment. If your members are very committed, no one can invite them away or steal them from you.

For I am persuaded, that neither death, nor life, nor angels, nor principalities, nor powers, nor things present, nor things to come, Nor height, nor depth, nor any other creature, shall be able to separate us from the love of God, which is in Christ Jesus our Lord.

Romans 8:38, 39

CHAPTER 9

How to Develop Devoted Members

A person goes through three stages when he is becoming established as a member of your church. As a shepherd, you must be able to distinguish between the different types of members that you have.

...he shall separate them one from another, as a shepherd divideth his sheep from the goats.

Matthew 25:32

3 Different Types of Members

1. Deer stage members

When a person is initially converted, he behaves like a deer: untamed, swift-footed and difficult to keep in one place. You have to track them down through the mountains and the forest. They are difficult to handle. It is important to move your members out of this stage. When you visit them, they play "hide-and-seek" with you. Deer are nimble creatures.

The Deer and the Assistant Deer

Seventeen years ago I visited a deer stage member called Adelaide. Somehow, she did not want to see her shepherd at all. This was one of the deer in my fellowship. I was trying to convert her from the deer stage to the sheep stage. I remember one evening when I knocked on her door in Volta Hall of the University of Ghana.

A voice from within answered, "Who is there?"

"It's me Brother Dag. I'm looking for Sister Adelaide."

After a few moments her roommate said, "Come in." This roommate happened to be her sister Irene.

"Hello. I am looking for Adelaide. Is she in?"

The roommate smiled sweetly, "Sorry, she's not in."

"Oh, I see. Where did she go?"

"I'm not sure, she just went out."

"Alright, please tell her I came by to check on her."

"Okay," she smiled again sweetly. "When she comes back I'll tell her you were here."

Each room had its own balcony, and unknown to me Adelaide was hiding there. I was a shepherd who was dealing with a deer and an assistant deer. Only deer dodge and hide. However, I worked on them until they became sheep. Today, they are stable "sheep" members.

2. Goat stage members

Goats are a little better than deer. They are far more domestic and easily accessible. However, a goat is much more independent than a sheep. They do what they want to do and are less likely to follow. When a church member graduates from the deer stage, they move on to the goat stage. As soon as a deer sees a human being, it takes off, whereas a goat remains. **Goats are friendlier than deer, though they can often have traces of stubbornness.**

3. Sheep stage members

Sheep are the best of the three groups. Your goal as a pastor should be to have your church full of devoted sheep. These people follow the shepherd. They stay together and move with the group. Such members are much easier to pastor. Sheep are often devoted, committed, faithful, dependable and loving members. If your church is full of devoted sheep, you will be a happy pastor. They will stay near you always, and receive your ministration.

Ten Keys for Developing Devoted Members

They devoted themselves to the instruction given by the apostles and to fellowship...

Acts 2:42 (Moffatt translation)

And they continued steadfastly in the apostles' doctrine and fellowship...

Acts 2:42

They devoted themselves to the apostles' teaching and to the fellowship...

Acts 2:42 (New International Version)

The number one task of a shepherd is to transform the members from deer to devoted sheep. How is this possible?

But we all...are changed into the same image from glory to glory...

2 Corinthians 3:18

Now the word "change" comes from a Greek word *metamorphoo,* which means metamorphosis. The word metamorphosis always reminds us of a dramatic transformation that occurs inside a cocoon when a larvae changes into a butterfly. When you see a butterfly elegantly fluttering around, you have no idea what it used to be like. There has been a drastic and major change – *metamorphosis.*

94

It is this same kind of *metamorphosis* that can take place in the members of a church. People change because of the ministry of the Word. They are transformed by the renewing of their minds. Loose and dodgy Christians can become devoted and committed zealots.

In this next section, I want to share with you a few keys on how to develop devoted membership. **The first important thing is that you the pastor, be devoted.** Devotion is a spiritual thing, it can be perceived. There are three main areas in which you can develop devoted membership: who you are, what you say and what you do.

1. Be a devoted pastor!

The pastor must be devoted to his church and his church members. Devotion is a spiritual thing. It is transmitted sometimes by osmosis – from person to person. *The unspoken commitment and sacrifice of the leadership is contagious; it passes from one member to another without speaking.* Why do I say this? Because not all pastors are committed to their churches.

I began my ministry as a medical student. In 1987, I was already struggling as a pastor/medical student. The tradition for newly qualified doctors in Ghana is for them to travel to America to seek "greener pastures". Medical doctors earn thousands of dollars in America, England and South Africa.

My fledgling church was full of people watching to see whether I would remain in Ghana or move out of the country. When the time came for the decision to be made, I declared boldly to my members that I was staying with them. I wasn't going to leave them. From that time onwards, I noticed a dramatic change in the commitment of the members to the church.

The sheep can sense the pastor's commitment. No one wants to follow someone who will abandon him midstream. In addition to the senior pastor being devoted, associates and assistants must be equally committed and devoted. The assistant pastors must be devoted to the senior pastor as well as to the church members.

The seed of devotion leads to a harvest of multiplied commitment from the church members.

2. Say positive things about the church.

Everybody wants to be part of a good thing. That is human nature. People are more likely to be devoted to something that is successful than to something that is failing. I have learnt that you can make your church flourish by *using your mouth*. If you want your church to grow, tell the members that they are part of a good church. Speak positively about the other pastors in the church. Do not criticize the pastors of the church.

That is why we call the Lighthouse Chapel International, *The Megachurch.* I am aware that this worries some people. It is just our faith confession! We know we have a long way to go. We know that we are still learning. But we believe that we have a mega ministry with a mega impact in a lost and dying world!

3. Say positive things about the pastors.

The associate pastor must say positive things about the senior pastor. He must say things like, "This is some of the best teaching you can get anywhere in the world." You must tell the church, "We are blessed to have such a man of God as our pastor." The Book of Acts, chapter two says that they continued steadfastly in the apostles' doctrine (teaching). One version puts it this way,

And they steadfastly persevered devoting themselves constantly...

Acts 2:42 (Amplified version)

You can make your church members become devoted to your teaching. Let them hear that it is the best they can get anywhere. The assistant pastor must constantly make the church aware of the precious gift that God has graciously given to them in their senior pastor.

I Am the Best Preacher for My Church

I believe I am the best preacher for my church. This is not vanity, it is biblical commonsense. I am their shepherd and I know what is best for my people. When God gives a woman a baby, He fills her breasts with milk for her baby. God does not fill another woman's breast with milk for that baby.

Similarly, God has filled my spirit with the Word of God for my sheep. My spiritual breasts are full of spiritual milk for my spiritual children. That is why I preach all the time to my church members. **I have other pastors, but I do ninety percent of the preaching and teaching. This is because I am the shepherd and God gave me the duty of feeding the sheep.**

Pastors ought to take charge of the pulpit and discharge their duties honourably. Thank God for visiting ministers. Many have ministered at my church and have been a blessing, but I am the best shepherd for my sheep.

In various ways, I make my church members become devoted to my teaching and preaching. I let them know that it's the best thing for them. If your members are not devoted to your preaching and teaching they will be devoted to someone else's ministry, and your church will not grow.

I have watched how visiting preachers are appreciated more than a resident pastor. This is unfortunate! Visiting pastors are often hailed as superheroes, whilst their resident pastors are ignored. The church members should not be deceived into thinking that the visiting minister has more to offer than their own pastor. He does not! He may have something different but he does not have anything better! It is only because the pastor from the church has fed the sheep so well, that there is a congregation groomed enough to receive a visiting minister.

One translation of Acts 2:42 says that they were devoted **"to the teaching of the apostles and to fellowship with one another."** In Bible times, the Christians were devoted to two principal things:

- **Their pastors' teachings.**

- **Fellowshipping with one another.**

Read Acts 2:42 for yourself! Read it from different versions of the Bible. It is crystal clear! Any simpleton should be able to understand these two strategic keys of church growth.

Get your church to be like the New Testament Church and you will have the thousands that are spoken of in the Book of Acts. **If you don't have an associate pastor who says good things about your teaching, then get one who does!**

4. Say good things about *your church members.*

In order to encourage inter-sheep relationships you must speak good things about your church members. Some people say things like, "I don't trust these church members." "I don't want any church member in my house." Although some church members may disappoint you, do not maintain a negative attitude towards all other members. That would be a big mistake!

I have heard Christians say, "I'd rather employ a Muslim than a Christian." That is unscriptural! The Bible teaches us to do good to Christians, especially your church members.

As we have therefore opportunity, let us do good unto all men, especially unto them who are of the household of faith.

Galatians 6:10

The fact that you have had unpleasant experiences with Christian men does not mean that you should marry an unbeliever. You are reacting in the wrong way. You are moving into foolishness!

Speak positively about Christians, especially your own church members. This will cause your church members to interact with each other. If you say evil things about them, new members will not form vital bonding relationships.

There is a principle at work here. **People are often attracted to the church by the pastor, but they often remain in the church because of the internal relationships they establish.** Never forget this! People stay in a church because of relationships they have in the church. It is the duty of the pastor to create interaction between members of the church.

This is a very important key to implement, if you really desire to have a large church. The Bible says that they were devoted to the fellowship. Members must be devoted to the fellowship of Christians in the same church. If you have members who hardly know each other, then introduce and influence them to develop relationships.

Encourage them to be committed to the church. Teach them that it is important to attend church all the time. **Teach them not to make a habit of hopping from church to church, just to see what is happening elsewhere.** Explain to them that it is only the devil who goes "to and fro" (Job 1:7).

5. Encourage employers to hire church members.

Practically speaking, you can also encourage the members to be devoted to one another's fellowship in many different ways. When I have a church member who is an employer in a strategic position, I encourage him to consciously help other members to get jobs. Do not think that this will happen naturally, the pastor's involvement is important.

When one Lighthouse member secures a job in a company, you will often find several other members finding their way there. Nowadays, this often happens naturally without my involvement. However, in the beginning I had to encourage this interaction. Many people were put off by the bad behaviour of some church members. Do not overreact to the disgraceful behaviour that some church members display when they are employed. Church members are human beings. Keep on recommending in the Spirit of love and forgiveness.

One employer said that he would not employ a member of the church because the church member would arrive at work late, claiming he went witnessing early in the morning. That is nonsense! Witnessing is not supposed to make you arrive late for work. I would encourage you to sack such a person. Church members are supposed to be disciplined!

6. Encourage members to apply for work from within the *church family.*

When you have a member who needs a job, direct him to other church members that can help him to get a job. This increases the members commitment because the sheep will see that you really care for them. The church then becomes an important family to belong to.

7. Encourage church members to marry each other.

Have you ever noticed how a young lady seems so committed to a church? Many of them have relationships within that church. Often it is their fiancés that act like glue which fixes them to the church. They are cemented to the church by their relationships. This is what I call *shepherdorial cement.* As I said earlier, they may be attracted initially to the church by the charismatic man of God, but they remain because of the relationships they acquire within the church!

I repeatedly tell my church members that the person they want to marry can be found within our congregation. If they want a tall, short, fat, skinny, fair or dark person; they can find their choice within the congregation! Of course, it is not a sin to marry from outside your own church. Many people in my church do that! All I am saying is that I encourage my church members to intermarry.

Anytime one of our "daughters", in whom we have invested, is married and taken to another church, we lose a church member. However, if this member stays on in the church, she will contribute to church growth. The couple will also have children who will become members of our children's church, and eventually our adult assembly. You may want to argue with my theory, but it's working very well for me!

8. Encourage members to *socialize* and *fraternize*.

The New Testament church was devoted to fellowshipping with one another! Sometimes people will accuse us of sticking to ourselves and not interacting with outsiders. However, that is not our intention at all! Our intention is also to interact with outsiders in order to win souls.

But make sure you encourage your church members to have their friends from within the church. **If your church members' friends are within the church, they will have two reasons for coming to church.** Firstly, they will come for spiritual nourishment. Secondly, they will come to meet with their friends. You can easily lose members whose friends are mainly people outside the church.

9. Develop smaller church families within the big church.

My church is made out of many small groups. Some groups have ten members, five, and even others have fifty.

It is these small groups, called ministries and fellowships, which form the nucleus of family relationships in our church. You may be surprised to discover that people are more committed to these smaller groups than to the big church. When there is a wedding or funeral, it is usually the concern of these smaller groups. Even when there is a social event, most of the friends are drawn out of these same groups.

10. Become a father or mother *to your church.*

Some pastors never develop beyond being a teacher of doctrines and truths. Chicks gather around the mother hen because of her motherly security.

> **...I have gathered thy children together, even as a hen gathereth her chickens under her wings...**
>
> **Matthew 23:37**

If you want your church to grow, develop fatherly or motherly attributes. Be everything to your sheep. Be a friend. Be a brother.

Be a father. Show concern for your flock. Show interest in things that concern them. Be interested in their school. Ask for details concerning their businesses. Help them in their marriages. Correct them when they are wrong. Rebuke them and discipline them when they need it. Don't just give them good teachings. Become a mother or a father to your flock. **The anointing to be a father or mother is the anointing to *gather*.**

To the weak became I as weak, that I might gain the weak: I am made all things to all men, that I might by all means save some.

1 Corinthians 9:22

CHAPTER 10

Retention Evangelism

One of the secrets of church growth is the secret of "retention evangelism". *Retention evangelism is the art of winning souls and retaining them.* Every pastor must learn to keep what he already has – at all costs.

...Gather up the fragments that remain, that nothing be lost.

John 6:12

Jesus did not waste any of His blessings. He wanted to save as much as He could.

The same applies to church growth. Our problem is not one of bringing new people to the church, but one of getting them to stay! If we can retain all the visitors and souls who come in through the front door, we will build a megachurch for Jesus.

A megachurch pastor is interested in what others despise. **Be interested in every single member.** Jesus collected the fragments.

If the fragments were important to the Lord, then the fragments must be important to you. Every member, big or small, rich or poor, must be important to you!

...Of them which thou gavest me have I lost none.

John 18:9

Let me share with you three vital strategies for retaining church members.

Three Vital Strategies for Retaining Church Members

Strategy 1: Follow-up Brings Retention

Many years ago, I learnt a simple truth which has stayed with me ever since. This truth has helped me greatly in the ministry. It is the secret of retention through follow-up.

My physics teacher once showed me a graph of the population of a poultry farm. The graph showed that the population of fowls remained constant at a low level for a long period. At a point, the fowls began to multiply and the farm population increased greatly. Something had happened to make the fowls multiply.

I then looked at the population of the world which had remained constant up until the beginning of the twentieth century. At the turn of the century, the population of the world began to expand greatly.

The question was: "What caused the sudden increase of the fowl population on the farm?" The other question was: "What made the population of the world increase so radically?"

The answer was simple. When the fowls in the poultry farm received the right medication and stopped dying from epidemics, the number of fowls suddenly increased. With the world's population, the pattern was the same. The reason for growth in the world's population was not the result of people having more babies. In fact, the number of births had been relatively the same. The reason for the growth was that the mortality rate had reduced. People's lifespan had been expanded due to medical science.

Medical science has improved remarkably from the beginning of the twentieth century. Diseases that have killed human beings for many years are now treated with one injection. Children no longer die from tuberculosis and malaria as they used to.

There is a great revelation to be derived from these two graphs! **If we can prevent a large number of converts from dropping out, then the church will experience the growth of the poultry farm.** If we can prevent many Christians from falling away, perhaps we will experience sudden accelerated growth like the world population did.

The Population/Follow-up Graph

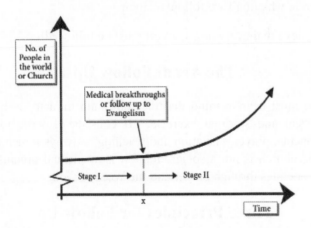

Stage I

® Mortality rate is high.

® No medicines, no medical answers.

® The growth of the population was very slow.

Stage II

® At time "x" there was a medical revolution.

® Mortality rate was greatly reduced: fewer people were dying.

® Suddenly, the population began to shoot up very rapidly.

® If a church is at Stage I, there is little or no growth. When a church begins follow-up, it is able to retain the people it gets from evangelism from a certain point "x" onwards. Notice how growth of the church occurs at Stage II.

This can be the graph of your church's membership. The turning point, as you can see, is the point at which retention begins. I see your church multiplying greatly in Jesus' name!

Every successful pastor must have the picture of this Follow-up Graph firmly imprinted in his spirit. The follow-up ministry is important because without it, our fasting and praying for church growth is in vain. Without follow-up, all of our efforts are useless! Without follow-up, all evangelism is worthless! Let's not make fools of ourselves. If we evangelize and invite people to church, why don't we follow them up?

I believe that every new convert must be followed-up.

The Art of Follow Up

You must bear in mind that the follow-up ministry is both a physical and spiritual exercise. It consists of three main components: prayer, visitation and teaching. Always remember that the church is not a social club. It is a spiritual organism, which operates through prayer and the Word of God.

Three Principles for Follow Up

1. Pray for visitors and converts

Pray that all visitors and converts will come back to the church. Declare that they will return the following week. Prophesy that when they go back home, they will return the next week with more people. Pray that when they return, they will come back with their families. Pray that they will become established in Christ! You travailed for them to be born again, now travail for Christ to be formed in them!

My little children, of whom I travail in birth again until Christ be formed in you.

Galatians 4:19

Without prayer, you are wasting your time. I really want to emphasize that prayer is important in order to achieve anything for the Kingdom of God. Pastors must emit spiritual energy whenever they speak or minister. Lead your entire church in prayer for the establishment of visitors and converts in the church.

2. Visit new converts and visitors

It is important to visit all new converts and visitors. This is an area where many of the church members can get involved. Churches are full of sleeping and lazy Christians who contribute nothing to the work of God. One person cannot effectively visit many people. However, one hundred trained workers can do a great deal more. I involve many people in following-up new converts.

There are three types of visits that church members must be trained to participate in.

Three Types of Visit

i. IDL visit

This is done to Identify and Locate the homes of converts. I encourage church members to accompany new converts to their homes after the service. This first visit is to locate their homes. Sometimes the official address does not correspond to the reality on the street. Physically going to homes for identification is a powerful first step in the visitation process.

ii. WELP visit

This visit is done to minister the Word. You must Encourage the new converts. This second visit will demonstrate that you really Love them. Finally, you must Pray with them for the establishment of their soul and for their general welfare.

iii. ABA visit

This involves *anagkazo, biazo* and *anaideia*. Sometimes you must visit your members and physically bring them with you to church. Demonstrate that you care by patiently waiting for them as they get ready for church, and take them to church. Many inactive Christians will become active if they find something to do in the church. Teach these three types of visitation for following-up new converts and you will discover how many more of your members will become active Christians.

3. Do Not Waste Your Time

You will have to be careful not to waste your time on non-serious converts. The Bible teaches us that we should commit things to faithful people. In other words, do not waste too much time on unfaithful people.

And the things that thou hast heard of me... commit thou to faithful men...

2 Timothy 2:2

The word faithful means constant and reliable. When a new convert says that he will be there and does not show up, this may be a sign of unfaithfulness. **Learn to distinguish between faithful and unfaithful converts. Then direct your time and investment to the faithful ones.**

On several occasions, I have wasted my time on non-serious converts (they probably weren't even born again). With time, I have learnt to distinguish between people who are serious with God and those who are just playing games. When you have many converts, you really have to learn to distinguish between who is serious and who is not. This is more crucial when your converts outnumber your lay workers. **In that case, you should only follow-up those who are serious.**

Strategy 2: Concentrate to Retain

Retention evangelism requires concentration. In every city, there are many different churches and pastors. Though many of these pastors and churches interact, they often end up having all sorts of conflicts. Unfortunately, in the real world, you will see competition between churches and pastors.

There will always be one or two pastors fighting for supremacy over the Body of Christ in their city. Who is the father and leader of us all? Some will claim, "I am the father and leader of all Christians in this city."

Others will take sides and join one faction or the other. I want to tell you right here, that your church will not grow if you involve yourself in these things.

Politics consumes both time and energy. **Church growth requires concentration.** The rays of the sun shine on us everyday, yet none of us catches fire. If you were to take a magnifying glass and concentrate the rays of the sun on one spot, you could set a piece of paper on fire. The principle at work here is the principle of concentration. *When the rays of the sun are not concentrated, they have no power to light a fire.*

Direct your spiritual energy towards your calling.

Our principal goal must be to fulfil the call of God on our lives. A prophet related a vision he had had to a friend of mine. He saw a world famous man of God standing on a platform.

Behind the platform were two electric generators. One of the generators was on and the other was off. The voice of God came loud and clear in this vision, "This man of God has neglected one half of his ministry." He had set aside the power and evangelistic dimension of his call and was only doing half of what he was called to do.

Two weeks after this revelation, this world famous man of God died suddenly. That was a real shock to everyone, including me. Failing to concentrate can cost you your church. It can cost you your ministry. It can even cost you your life!

Strategy 3: Devotion Brings Retention

Another essential method for retaining your membership is to teach devotion in the church. You must teach them to be devoted to the pastor's teachings. You must teach them to be devoted to one another's fellowship. We have discussed this at length in a previous chapter.

It is also very important for the pastor to be devoted to his members. When a pastor is devoted to his members it leads to retention. Anytime there is a wedding, funeral, baby dedication or some crisis in your church member's life, you have a chance to practise devotion. That is your golden opportunity to devote yourself to your sheep. Stand by them at the graveside. Be there in their deepest sorrow. Attend their important events.

This demonstrates your devotion to them. You are fulfilling a principle: whatsoever a man sows he shall reap. **You will reap the devoted membership of your church members.** Many years ago I heard a seasoned pastor say, "If you stand by your members in their time of need, they will stand by you in yours."

CHAPTER 11

How to Have Permanent Church Members

The Lord emphasized to me the need to have permanent church members. I realized that many of the young church members were vacillators. **The best type of church member is a permanent church member.** A permanent member is unmovable, stable and dependable throughout the years. A very important characteristic of that member is that his mind and heart are saying, *"I am here, and I am here forever."*

I am not a fool! Of course I know that not everybody is going to stay forever. Yet, it is important for people to have the mind of staying around forever. I am not God. If God, by His Spirit, would lead someone away from our church, there is nothing I can do about it. It is the same thing with marriage. No good person enters a marriage with the mind that "I am in this marriage for just a few years. Who would like to marry such a person?

My Famous Announcement

One day I told my church, "I have decided to go to America to study cardiothoracic surgery." I announced, "I am going to be a heart surgeon."

I went on to explain, "The course will last for about five years after which I will need to gain some experience on the job. That will last for another five years, making the trip a total of ten years."

The whole congregation was shocked. "Ooooooh," they said, "It can't be possible." They all looked very sad.

"Why are you sad?" I asked, "Don't you want me to go away?"

I asked them, "How many of you would like me to be here in three years' time?" Everybody raised their hands.

I asked again, "How many of you here would like me to be here in seven years' time?" Again, they all raised their hands.

"So you don't want me to go," I said.

They all shouted, "No!"

I began to laugh. Then I told them, "I was just joking. I'm glad you want me to stay! I realize that you want me to stay permanently!"

I went on, "If you would like me to be here in seven years' time, I would also like you to be here seven years from now. Just as you want me to be your permanent pastor, preaching to you and praying for you, I also want you to be permanent members for me!"

I believe in permanent members and permanent commitment. I would strongly recommend all pastors to teach their congregations about being permanently joined to the church. Listen to me, faith comes by hearing and hearing by the Word of God (Romans 10:17). *What you teach your people is what they will believe.* If you want them to be a permanent part of the ministry, teach them and they will be!

The church members want a permanent pastor and we the pastors want permanent members. I am going to give you several reasons that you can share with any congregation as to why they should become permanent members of the church. If you teach these things, your members will stop jumping around from church to church.

Eleven Reasons Why Your Congregation Must Be Permanent Members

1. They are part of a family.

Of whom the whole family in heaven and earth is named...

Ephesians 3:15

The first reason why people must be permanent part of the church is because they are part of a family. When every church member is taught that the church is a family, they will be less willing to leave. Every family has its problems! In every family, you have conflicts and misunderstandings. But there is simply no way you can leave your family. You are simply a part of that family whether you like it or not.

A misunderstanding with your uncle does not lead you to change your name. Teach the church members that misunderstandings and hurts should not make them change their churches. Family members belong together in a lifetime commitment. Church members must belong to the same family in a lifetime commitment.

2. They are part of a building.

For we are labourers together with God: ye are God's husbandry, ye are God's building.

1 Corinthians 3:9

The second reason why people need to be permanent is because they are part of God's building. The Bible clearly teaches that we are God's building. Every Christian must know that he is part of God's building, which is the church. You cannot easily remove the blocks of a building. Blocks are a permanent part of the structure. **How would you feel if you came home**

113

and your bedroom had moved to the next house? Sections of buildings do not move around!

I teach my church to see themselves as permanent building blocks in the building called Lighthouse Chapel International. I tell them that I have never seen a building block walk out of a building before. Such an occurrence would be magical. I trust that there is no magician amongst the members.

3. They are part of a garden.

And now go to; I will tell you what I will do to my vineyard: [garden] I will take away the hedge thereof, and it shall be eaten up; and break down the wall thereof, and it shall be trodden down...

Isaiah 5:5

Throughout Scripture, we see believers being referred to as a garden. If we are like a garden, then each of us is like a plant in the garden. If you uproot a plant and replant it in another spot, you endanger the life of that shrub. In fact, if you do this repeatedly, you will kill the plant.

It is a common fact that planting and replanting kills plants. God has no plan for planting and replanting His people in different churches every few years. If every time your roots go a little deeper you move around, you will kill yourself spiritually. I have noticed that Christians who are planted and replanted in different churches often do not survive spiritually.

When the Lord asked the devil where he had been, the devil replied that he had been roaming in the earth. The devil does not sit still, he moves "to and fro" and "up and down" in the earth. If you move to and fro, from church to church, your lifestyle resembles the devil.

And the Lord said unto Satan, Whence comest thou? Then Satan answered the Lord, and said, From going

to and fro in the earth, and from walking up and down in it.

Job 1:7

4. **They are part of a tree.**

I am the vine, ye are the branches: He that abideth in me, and I in him, the same bringeth forth much fruit: for without me ye can do nothing.

John 15:5

Another important revelation is that you are a part of a tree. Jesus said that He is the vine and we are the branches. Everyone knows that a branch cut off from the tree is dead. Branches are intended to be permanently fastened to bigger branches or tree trunks.

If you are indeed a branch, have no plans of moving anywhere. People who move from church to church often do not flourish in the Kingdom of God. They experience stunted growth and some even backslide and go to Hell.

Pastor Turns Rasta

Recently I was speaking with a prophet of God. He told me how the Lord had shown him a dream, about how a pastor who had been moving from church to church, had backslidden and had become a Rastafarian. This prophetic dream was predicting that the vacillating pastor was going to fall. This was a warning to the unstable pastor.

Cutting yourself off and attempting to re-attach yourself is risky business. I believe in permanent membership. I teach permanent membership. I campaign for permanent members. *My people want a permanent pastor, and I want permanent members.*

5. They will flourish if they are planted.

Those that be planted in the house of the Lord shall flourish in the courts of our God.

Psalm 92:13

The next reason for permanent membership is so that you will flourish. You will notice that I have a scriptural basis for each of these points. What I am sharing with you is sound biblical doctrine. I am not saying that there are no grounds for a person to leave a church. Not at all! What I'm saying is that you must teach people to be permanently attached and permanently planted for their own benefit. Sheep will follow and obey what their shepherd tells them.

The Bible tells us plainly that those who are planted will flourish. I have watched Christians and pastors who move around from place to place. **You cannot compare a planted member to a roving member.** Stay in one place. Develop roots and flourish!

As you remain in one place, you will develop businesses and business contacts. Members of the church will begin to rely on you for their business. You will develop lasting friendships that may help you during your lifetime. Staying in one place for only a couple of years does not allow you to develop the sort of relationships that you need for a blessed life.

6. They can invest freely when they are permanent.

It is very convenient to live in one's own house. It is very different from renting a house. When you live in your own house, you can invest freely. You can pour in your money, your time and your life. Why is this? Because it is yours and you are going to be there permanently. No one wants to spend any money on a house that doesn't belong to him. After all, he is only going to use the place for a few months.

When we acquired our own church building, we invested freely into the structure. One day the contractor told me, "I want to construct this building as perfectly as possible because I am going to be here for life."

"I want the floor to be smooth and perfect because I intend to die as a member of Lighthouse," he added.

He continued, "One day when I am dead and my coffin is being carried into the church for the funeral service, I will not want anyone to trip and fall over an uneven floor."

I laughed. Though this was a joke, he was also making a serious point. He had planned to be there for life. In other words, he had opted for permanent membership.

Permanent members will be encouraged to give their money freely. They know that they are building a church for their children's weddings and will see the fruit of their investments.

7. They will have a family to *celebrate their victories.*

I preach faith and hope for the future. I tell my members that things are going to get better. Many poor people come to the church. As they hear the Word, their faith rises and they begin to see better things ahead.

If they are permanent members, they will live to celebrate their victories in the church. If they are not permanent, in the day of their victory, they will have no one to rejoice with. *Remember that joy shared is double joy and sorrow shared is half sorrow.*

Rejoice with them that do rejoice...

Romans 12:15

They will have a family to rejoice with as their new houses, new cars and new babies are dedicated. You will stand together and remember how the Lord took them from the beginning and brought them so far!

I have often reminisced with my friends about the ministry. We ponder over how the Lord has been kind to us. We laugh about things that threatened us some years ago. We say like the psalmist,

> **When the Lord turned again the captivity of Zion, we were like them that dream. Then was our mouth filled with laughter, and our tongue with singing: then said they among the heathen, The Lord has done great things for them.**
>
> **Psalm 126:1, 2**

Who will you sit down with to quote this Scripture to one day? Will you have abandoned all the friends with whom you struggled in the early days? A permanent relationship will give you people to rejoice with in the day of rejoicing. Better days are ahead. I teach my church that our better days are yet to come. I want them to stay around to see the better days of this ministry.

I remember when I used to speak about miracles. It was more like a dream. Today we have real miracles abounding in our midst. The Lord has been good to us. We are seeing better days. When you are permanent, you will have a family to go through your mourning with you. Joy shared is double joy, and sorrow shared is half sorrow.

8. They will see the fruit of *their labour.*

It is important for Christians to know that harvest time is coming in the future. What is the use of labouring in a church for years, only to leave just before harvest time? Some of the people who were with me in the days of real struggles are no longer around to enjoy the blessings. That is a pity! That is the price you pay for not being permanent.

Anyone who is double-minded about his commitment becomes unstable in other areas of his life. The Bible states that such a person is unstable in *all* his ways. Be stable. Be permanent. Be blessed.

> **A double minded man is unstable in all his ways.**
>
> **James 1:8**

9. They will avoid the deception of *short relationships.*

Short relationships are sweet while they last. There are no quarrels, no emotional disturbances, no worrying comments or misunderstandings. Long relationships have often been through much testing.

Long relationships that have survived the tests of time are better. Greater trust develops. You also know what to expect in the relationship. I prefer to work with someone I have known for a long time rather than with someone I have just met.

Joshua Made That Mistake!

Joshua made the mistake of forming an alliance with someone he didn't really know. He thought the Gibeonites were ambassadors from a far country.

Little did he know that they had lied to him in order to secure a peace treaty. He later discovered their true identity. But it was too late! He was already bound to the peace accord, although it was done under a cover of deception.

...And Joshua said unto them, Who are ye? and from whence come ye? And they [Gibeonites] said unto him, From a very far country... And it came to pass at the end of three days after they had made a league with them, that they heard that they were their neighbours, and that they dwelt among them.

Joshua 9:8, 9, 16

What I am saying is that longer relationships are safer relationships. Permanent members will be able to develop genuine relationships with genuine people. As the years go by, the members will know whether they have a genuine pastor or not and they will be more committed.

10. They will have consistent *pastoral care.*

The church, like a hospital, cares for you. Your permanent pastor can cater for you better because he has been with you for

119

a long time and knows your history better. He is better equipped to minister to you.

Church members often leave churches when they think the pastor has discovered their secret sins. You must want your pastor to have access to your life so that he can minister in the area where you really need help.

11. They will be rewarded for faithfulness.

The next important reason for being a permanent member is that God will reward His children for faithfulness.3 Faithfulness means loyalty, constancy and permanence.

> **Well done, good and faithful servant...enter thou into the joy of thy Lord.**
>
> **Matthew 25:23**

Please note in this scripture that, the servant is recommended for his faithfulness. He is not recommended for his charisma or his gifting. Being a permanent member is part of the life of faithfulness. Be faithful. Be permanent. One day, Jesus will tell you, "Enter thou into the joy of thy Lord." That is the day I am waiting for. I just want to hear Him say, "Well done, good and faithful (permanent and loyal) servant!"

CHAPTER 12

The Secret of Industrialization

I like to think of the future and how things will be like in some years to come. I have often wondered what our church will be like in a few years. As I pondered over the future of the church, the Lord told me that one way I could secure the future was to develop a culture of industrialization.

God instructed me to industrialize my church. He showed me how our nation, at that time, was only importing goods from western countries and reselling them at a profit. "There is no future in this," the Lord said. "Have you noticed that the richest nations of the world are all involved in producing important products?"

"Yes," I replied. God showed me that the richest nations of the world produce cars. The best cars come from the richest countries of the world. These countries are rich because they produce something. The church will be rich in souls if we begin to be spiritually industrialized!

Just as the success of the nations of the world depends on their producing something, the success of the church depends on her producing souls. An industry is an organized system of producing goods and services regularly.

An industry is a deliberately (intentionally) organized system. It comes out with a well-defined product on a regular basis. It does not only produce its products when it is convenient nor does it produce goods accidentally. An industry is also very profit-oriented. Any nation that does not establish industries is doomed to buy secondhand things forever. It is doomed to be at the mercy of those who produce goods and services.

When I speak of industrialization, I am not speaking of making money. I am talking about churning out souls deliberately and regularly. I am a "businessman" for God, and my currency is human souls. Your church will have reached an industrialized stage when it begins to churn out souls regularly and systematically. The important word here is regular. I know of some car factories that produce one car every three minutes.

Jesus said in Luke 19:13, "Occupy (do business) till I come." That is, industrialize and commercialize with diligence until I come. In other words, Jesus expects us to take the business of soul winning as a very serious enterprise. Soul winning should be intentional and not incidental.

Many pastors are afraid of starting churches because they do not know how to win souls. Others don't know how to follow-up and establish converts in the Lord. They only know how to break churches and take away half of somebody's church members. No industry turns out a car accidentally. It is a deliberate planned exercise. It is time for us to deliberately win souls with the regularity of a factory.

God showed me how to set up the church and ministry to deliberately and regularly win souls every month. My church is divided into chapels, ministries and fellowships. Each ministry is supposed to have a regular monthly outreach.

The Lord showed me that it is important for the ministries to develop the habit of having a monthly outreach without needing a special exhortation to do so. Car factories do not need a charismatic manager to preach about the importance of producing their product for the month! In contrast, churches and ministries seem to need a special emotional seminar on soul winning. Without this, everybody forgets about the harvest. Surely this is not an industrialized church.

That is why I initiated ministries and fellowships, so that we would win some souls every month. I am not directly involved in the winning of those souls. It is done at the ministry and fellowship level. I do not have to go and whip up enthusiasm for the winning of souls before it happens. It just happens automatically.

An industry is profit-conscious.

Again, the kingdom of heaven is like unto a merchant man, seeking goodly pearls [souls]:

Matthew 13:45

An industrialized church is concerned with the number of people converted every month. It is biblical to be interested in the number of souls that are being added to the church daily, weekly or monthly.

...And the Lord added to the church daily such as should be saved.

Acts 2:47

It is interesting to note how many pastors rarely do altar calls. Many ministers do not care about the lost souls. Instead, they care about how impressive they were and how powerfully they ministered!

After ministering at a convention, the host pastor said something to me that struck my heart. He said, "You are the only minister who made an altar call during this convention." I asked myself, "Have altar calls for salvation become obsolete?" How sad! The primary job of the church is being relegated to the background.

Altar calls for salvation are compulsory in every service we have. I make altar calls at all weddings and funerals. Industrialize your church – regularly and deliberately conduct outreaches. I see you increasing as you industrialize your church!

When a church is industrialized, even when the charismatic leader is no more, the church will continue to grow on its own accord. Why industrialize? So that we may increase and not diminish.

Build ye houses, and dwell in them; and plant gardens, and eat the fruit of them; Take ye wives, and beget sons and daughters; and take wives for your sons, and give your daughters to husbands, that they may bear sons and daughters; that ye may be increased there, and not diminished.

Jeremiah 29:5, 6

CHAPTER 13

Principles for Church Growth

The following are principles that I have discovered for building successful and large churches. I advise you to carefully consider them and allow the Lord to give you a deeper understanding of what I am teaching in this chapter.

Fourteen Principles for Church Growth

1. The principle of the multiplied senior pastor

I have discovered that if you could multiply the senior pastor by twelve, it would mean that you had twelve pastors at work. Logically, you could do twelve times as much work. I taught my assistant pastors to do whatever I do. If I meet people after church, they should also meet people after church. If I am able to counsel ten people and twelve other pastors are able to counsel ten people, that makes it one hundred and thirty people who are being attended to.

There are some churches in which the senior pastor is a "superman". He is the only one who does anything important – and that is a sure recipe to keep your church small. One person can only attend to a certain number of people. If you try to visit, counsel and help everybody, you will go crazy!

There is a limit to what you can do. That is why I have many branches and many pastors. I believe that many of the people I preach to can also preach. I believe that many of the people who are receiving the Word now, are capable of rising up into the ministry.

Do not be an insecure senior pastor. Don't be afraid to trust people. It is true that many people will betray your trust, but if you live in fear, Satan will have access to your life and ministry. I have been hurt by some people, but I have decided to still trust others to help me. If they betray me one day, I will take it in stride and keep on trusting some others.

One of the reasons why some people cannot trust is because they do not believe that people can do a good enough job. In the medical field, young doctors are being trained all the time. Some people are always attended to by inexperienced student doctors under supervision. As the young doctors are allowed to have a go, they learn and soon they are just as good. It is the same thing in the ministry. People must be trusted with responsibilities under supervision. **They must be allowed to do important things.** This will multiply the number of capable pastors in the ministry.

2. The principle of maximized Sunday usage

This principle has been stretched to its fullest at the Lighthouse Cathedral in Accra. The principle of using Sunday to its fullest is effective because traditionally, people have dedicated Sunday to both resting and going to church. Since so many of the church members are available on Sunday, it is only wise to use Sunday to its fullest. Sunday is a full working day for me. Jesus worked on Sundays and I would like to follow His example.

And therefore did the Jews persecute Jesus, and sought to slay him, because he had done these things on the sabbath day. But Jesus answered them, My father worketh hitherto, and I work.

John 5:16, 17

Sunday is a full working day for all lay pastors in our church. We work hard from Sunday morning until late Sunday evening. We are able to accomplish a lot of counselling because people are free on Sundays. Visitation is also very effective on Sundays because many people are at home on Sunday afternoons. We conduct Bible schools for lay people on Sunday afternoons. Many people are able to attend because they don't have much to do on Sundays.

Decide to utilize your Sundays. I don't know what pastors are doing in their homes at two o'clock on Sunday afternoon when most of the church members are available to be ministered to. Take advantage of this opportunity. Lay pastors and shepherds will be able to do more work for the Lord.

Although some people find it difficult to accept, I emphasize to all the people I work with, that Sunday is a full working day for me and my church. I am not an accountant or a computer programmer. My working hours are not Monday to Friday from nine to five. I work on Sundays and I rest on Mondays. We do not start work at eight o'clock in the morning. I see no reason to go to work at eight o'clock in the morning. We stay late in the evenings because that is when many lay people are available for us to minister to them.

Our office is usually closed on Mondays, and all of our staff, except the security officers, have a day off. Pastors and churches must not allow the world to impose its schedule on us. When airplane pilots go to work at odd hours no one complains. Everyone accepts that their work demands a different type of work schedule. Pastors and non-pastoral people must realize that the work of the ministry is peculiar and goes with its own special working hours.

Begin to consider what you can do with your Sundays. Think of how many more people you can attend to if your Sundays are used for ministry instead of being used for sleeping and having lunches in the afternoon.

3. The principle of smaller sub-divisions

Smaller sub-divisions within the church allow for better pastoral care, which eventually leads to church growth. Questions that cannot be asked in a large Sunday service can be addressed in the small groups. The small groups become the family units to which church members belong.

I have several smaller groups within the church. I have always believed that every Christian can and should actively serve the Lord. These smaller groups allow for all Christians to get involved.

As your church becomes mega, it will remain small enough to meet the needs of all the people. As it is said, "Large enough to include you, and small enough to know you."

Some people's churches are like large convention centres. People come in, hear the Word, and go away. No human being likes to feel that he is not known. People are not numbers they are human beings. **Nobody wants to be reduced to a numbered article or a countable commodity.** People want to feel important. People want to feel necessary. People want to feel loved. You may preach a powerful sermon but, they still need to belong to a little family.

Your church can be broken into cells, divisions or departments. Our church has chapels, ministries and fellowships. I am always encouraging my members to get involved in one ministry or the other. How can I know all the people who come to church? How can I know what they think or feel? How can I know their problems and how can I help them?

If you think that God is going to give you a word of knowledge about these people everyday, you are making a mistake. God expects you to break up your church into smaller divisions so that the people can receive adequate pastoral care.

4. The principle of the Person X oriented church

What on earth is a "person x" oriented church? I define "person x" as a new convert or a new member. **Most churches are oriented towards established members.** A "person x" oriented church is very concerned about new people and visitors.

Treat your visitors well. We make song sheets so that the new people can get involved during the praise and worship. After the service, we host a reception to allow our new members to feel at home. We also give gifts to new converts.

Recently, the Lord directed me to direct my most senior associates to handle all new converts. God told me that if new converts were important to me, then I should allow senior ministers to take care of them rather than junior leaders. This has helped tremendously to establish many new people in the church. When a church is "person x" oriented, it is on the road towards increase because, growth will come through new members and converts.

> **And those members of the body, which we think to be less honourable, upon these we bestow more abundant honour...**

> **1 Corinthians 12:23**

Most people think that growth comes because more people visit the church. This is not necessarily the case. Some people also think that growth takes place because more converts are won. History has shown that the population of this world has increased because people are being kept alive and not because more people are being born. If we want our churches to grow, we have to sustain and maintain our new members and converts.

5. The principle of catering for group A and group B members

Every church can be divided into group A and group B members. Group A members are the more reliable people; they attend church twice or more a week. They are often involved in other small group activities in the church life. Thank God for Group A members. We really appreciate their input.

Group B members on the other hand, are the once-a-weekers, non-small group members, early service lovers, short sermon lovers, mind drifters, day dreamers, Bible forgetters, non note-takers, non tithe payers, clock-watchers and the church-near-me attendees.

These group B members will form an important segment of your church, as it becomes a larger entity. You will have to accept them as part of the family. **You can choose your friends, but you cannot choose your brothers.** Not everybody is going to be a prayer warrior.

In fact, in a large church many of the people fall into group B. Love them anyway. Preach sermons that they can also appreciate. Pray for them. The Spirit of the Lord will work on them. Sometimes when you organize a social event like a beach party, the group B members will flood the place. Use such opportunities to minister to them.

If you try to filter out your group B members, you may be left with nothing at the end of the day. Jesus said that the harvest is plenteous but the laborers are few. Jesus didn't say that there were few members, He said that there were few labourers (Group A members).

6. The principle of multiple services

Nobody ever told me that multiple services lead to church growth. I discovered it almost by accident. Well, now I am telling you that multiple services lead to church growth.

We have seven different services every Sunday morning. It is very tiring and draining, but our church attendance is better because of these multiple services. As the church grows, people with all sorts of needs come into the church.

Some pastors give the impression that they conduct multiple services because they have such a large crowd. This is true to some extent. But I do not have multiple services because the building can be filled four times over. Not all the services are full. Each service has a different level of attendance. I have never seen multiple services where all the services have the same attendance. **I conduct multiple services primarily to make a variety of convenient services available to my members.**

I am always amazed at why people will want to come to church at 6 o'clock in the morning. I always ask myself, "Can't they come to church a little later?" Human beings are so varied. **Once you are dealing with a large number of people you are dealing with variety.** If you don't make variety available, you will lose those for whom you have nothing to offer.

Accept the reality of variety and flow with it. You will notice that different types of people come to each service. Some of the services are more formal whilst others are more relaxed. The type of people who attend each service determines the type of atmosphere you get. We have services for the youth and for the children. We have services for different languages. We have several services for English speaking members. Each of these services is different and there are people to fit into all of these services. **God will bless your church as you provide variety for more people.**

7. The principle of dynamic church services

You must have a goal for each service you conduct. When determining the goal of the service, you must ask yourself, "What am I trying to achieve with this service?" Are you planning to raise the dead, to heal the sick, or to preach and teach? In the Lighthouse Cathedral, our Sunday morning services are teaching and worship services. We do not usually pray for the sick on Sunday mornings. We pray for the sick on other days.

How much time have you allotted for each service? How long should the service be? Our services are one and a half hours and two hours each. Within two hours, you can do everything that you need to do for a church service.

Many years ago, I attended a church whose services began around eight o'clock in the morning and ended at about three o'clock in the afternoon. After attending twice, I decided that the service was too long. Today, that church is non-existent. When your Sunday services are too long, you will drive away all of your members. You cannot achieve everything on a Sunday morning. We conduct miracle services which can last for several hours. We have camp meetings at which I can preach for more than twelve hours in a day. At the last Shepherd's Camp Meeting of my church. I preached from 6:30 a.m. to 12:30 a.m. on one of the days with only two short breaks. I know how to have long meetings, but I'd advise you not to use your Sunday services for such things.

What type of meeting place do you have? Man looks on the outward appearance, so it is important to decorate your church nicely. Even if you do not own a church building, let your place of meeting attain a certain standard. **Remember that you have only one chance to give a first impression.** Make use of flowers, baskets, curtains or anything that would improve the physical appearance.

Sometimes the pastor does not have very good taste. How can you know if you do not have good taste? He would have to rely on others in the church to help in enhancing and brightening his corner.

It is important that every church tries to acquire its own place of meeting. Owning your own facility introduces more stability to the church.

How do you present yourself? God looks on the heart, but man looks on the outward appearance. Man cannot see your heart. Man can only see your outward appearance. That is why your outward appearance is also important. We must seek to put up a good outward appearance in addition to preparing the right heart for the Lord. Everyone who plays a part in the service must be well dressed. Male pastors must be formally dressed and neatly shaved. Female pastors must be properly dressed and must not wear suggestive or indecent clothing.

In some churches the musicians look like agents from the world who have been temporarily contracted to help God. These instrumentalists often come in with the attitude and culture of secular pop groups. That is why I insist on all my musicians dressing like pastors. If they cannot afford it, we buy clothes for them!

Altar calls should be made at every service. This important and good habit must be maintained at all costs. New converts and visitors must receive a warm welcome. Remember these are the "person x" members. The assisting pastor should take over and briefly emphasize the message of the senior pastor. He should also encourage the congregation to buy tapes.

Pastors must not run off after church. They must stay and mingle with the congregation for some time after the service. I question the call of someone who says he's a pastor but does not want to mingle with his congregation after the service. The shepherd's place is in the field amongst the sheep. **A true shepherd smells of sheep.** I remember meeting a frustrated congregant in a church. This man had travelled many miles to attend a conference. He wanted to have a chance to say hello to the great man of God. He was so frustrated that he became bitter. I met him in a lift and he said to me bitterly, *"Is this man a prime minister or a pastor?"*

But I have been to other conferences where the men of God made the effort to stay around and mingle with the sheep. Some people just want to shake your hand. Give them the opportunity to get near if you can. A pastor's wife must help with the interaction and must be seen to be a warm and friendly person. All these things contribute to building the mega church we all desire.

8. The principle of using technology and research

As the number of passengers on different airlines has increased, their efficiency has improved. This is because air line industries have used technology to help them in their work. Whilst the membership of most churches has increased over the past few years, the pastor's ability for handling larger crowds has not been developed.

In our church, we try to keep an accurate data and statistics department. We maintain accurate counts and figures of everything. We have developed our own pastoral care monitoring system which we call the "Pastoshep".

In spite of the limitations due to limited addresses and telephone numbers in Ghana, our Pastoshep has become a reliable and technological method of assessing the work of all pastors and shepherds alike. Without being there to physically see what people are doing, my computer tells me what everybody is doing. I decided long ago to allow technology to help me to do the work of God.

Too many pastors say things like, "The whole of the outside was full." They say things like, "Thousands of people were here today." Whereas in reality, just a few hundred were present. Let's have real numbers!

We sometimes do surveys in the church to find out different interesting things. For instance, we did a survey to find out how many members of the church had ever been visited by a pastor. The results of that study were certainly revealing!

9. The 80-20 principle

This rule teaches us that eighty percent of your increase comes from twenty percent of the people. This means that eighty percent of church growth is as a direct result of the work of twenty percent of your members. Therefore, it is important for every pastor to spend more time with the twenty percent who will bring church growth.

Often the leaders, teachers and pastors make up this twenty-percent. They are the most important people in the church. More time, personal interaction and prayer with this twenty percent will give you amazing results that you never expected. Some pastors spend most of their time with the rich and influential. They do not know that they are spending time with the wrong group. **Spending time with rich people does not make your church grow.** It rather makes the rich people more important than they really are. It can make the rich people stubborn and difficult to pastor!

A church with a future will identify potential leaders and put them to work. When you do

this, you are looking out for the twenty percent who can bring about sustained church development.

When I visit our churches outside the headquarters, I spend more time with the leaders and pastors than with the rest of the church. Often I just minister in one service. Afterwards, I have various meetings, spending several hours with the pastors and shepherds. This style of activity does not come naturally. It is born out of the knowledge of the 80-20 Principle.

When you implement the 80-20 Principle, you may initially think that you are doing the wrong thing, but that is not the case. You will soon discover that this simple principle is a secret of church growth.

10. The principle of the scholarly pastor

By this, I simply mean that pastors should develop themselves academically. I have never been to Bible school; I only attended medical school. Yet, I have learnt so much about the ministry by reading.

I always have several books that I am reading at the same time. I believe in reading, studying and acquiring knowledge. How could I rise above the handicap of having no formal pastoral training? Only by reading!

There is a difference between ministers who read books and those who do not. **Those who do not read are no better than those who cannot read! Those who do not read are doomed to be ruled by those who do read.** Paul the apostle was a reader of books and parchments. He deemed his books so important that he asked Timothy to bring them to him.

...when thou comest, bring with thee, and the books, but especially the parchments.

2 Timothy 4:13

Prophet Daniel read the books that Jeremiah wrote.

In the first year of his reign, I Daniel understood by books the number of the years, whereof the word of the Lord came to Jeremiah the prophet, that he would accomplish seventy years in the desolations of Jerusalem.

Daniel 9:2

People like Daniel and Paul read books. It is no surprise that they went far in ministry. There are many ministers who also need some secular education. They would do well to educate themselves in important subjects like administration, law, medicine and history. Administration is important in a church because many aspects of the church have to be run in a secular way. Things have to be managed properly. Accounts have to be prepared. Salaries have to be determined and paid. People have to be employed and dismissed. Things simply have to be done properly. A good study of administration and management will do the church of God a lot of good.

The study of law is also important for pastors and churches. Churches enter into contracts and the law of contract becomes important. There are laws that affect property acquisition. The law of property then becomes important to the pastor. There are laws that concern marriage. Pastors have to be well versed in the laws that exist. God does not want His ministers to be ignoramuses. I am not a lawyer, but I know quite a bit about law because I have taken an interest in it for my own sake.

A good understanding of medicine is also important. A pastor, like a doctor, often deals with terminally ill people. There is no use in a pastor not appreciating the conditions of their members. It is important to have a basic understanding of what is going on around you. I have seen pastors declaring healing based on ridiculous and presumptuous premises. How absurd we sometimes look to the professionals of this world! They know we are completely unlearned in certain areas.

Another area that pastors need a bit of education in is history and politics. History shows the rise and the fall of tyrants. It shows trends which keep repeating themselves. The Bible says that there is nothing new under the sun. In fact, the Bible predicts that the past will repeat itself over and over again. For those of you who want to know the future – it is basically the past repeated.

The thing that hath been, it is that which shall be; and that which is done is that which shall be done: and there is no new thing under the sun. Is there anything whereof it may be said, See, this is new? it hath been already of old time, which was before us.

Ecclesiastes 1:9, 10

11. The principle of having a power ministry

If you cut out all the Scriptures on healing and miracles from your Bible, you will discover that your Bible is totally destroyed! You will be destroying the Word of God. When you take out the Scriptures concerning the power of God, you are left with a book on philosophy.

It is not only the teaching and preaching which helps God's people. God's children also want to receive a touch of His power. **It is important to add on the power dimension of miracles, healings and deliverance.** The Holy Spirit wants to manifest Himself and bless the people of God. You will discover that your people love to be prayed for. It is important for you to pray for your sheep and minister God's power to them.

12. The principle of pastoral individuality: fulfil your call.

It is very important for every pastor to fulfil his individual call. Don't look to the crowd. Don't think about what others are doing.

Many years ago when I started out in ministry, many people laughed at me. One pastor ridiculed me as I encouraged my members to go out and witness door-to-door. He sneered at me and said, "What is witnessing? What is door-to-door witnessing? We have moved on into higher realms of ministry!"

I answered, "It is an important Christian activity."

I stressed, "No matter how big you become in the ministry, it is important to preach the gospel from house-to-house."

Today, that pastor who scoffed at me is struggling at the bottom of the ministerial ladder. Please do not allow anyone to drown your convictions. Be a man of conviction. Follow the plan that God has given to you. Comparison is one of the dangerous practices of certain ministers. Please do not compare yourself with anyone else, it is too dangerous.

For we dare not make ourselves of the number, or compare ourselves with some that commend themselves: but they, measuring themselves by themselves, and comparing themselves among themselves, are not wise.

2 Corinthians 10:12

God told me not to compare myself with anybody. He showed me how certain ministers were uneducated and that His expectations of different people varied. He also showed me that my background of prolonged education made Him give me a different standard. He told me that I would be wrong to compare myself with anyone else. The Lord also showed me that if I used other ministers as a standard, I may do far less for Him than I am supposed to. The Lord showed me that I would mistakenly think that I had "arrived" because I had used certain low standards that had been set by others. It is indeed a dangerous thing to compare yourselves with others. Paul said that he dared not compare himself with others.

13. The principle of massive organized prayer

Massive organized prayer involves gathering all of your leaders and/or members for intensive prayer. I do massive organized prayer on three levels. At the highest level, I frequently organize the senior ministers away from the city to pray for a few days.

At the level of cell leaders, we often decree what we call prayer sentences. Sometimes we "sentence" the shepherds to twenty hours of prayer within a three-week period. This means that they have to meet as a group and pray for twenty hours spread over three weeks. This is massive organized prayer – organizing prayer on a massive scale.

Finally, we involve the whole church in prayer. There are times we have all-night prayer and fasting meetings everyday for an entire week. I am always surprised when on a weekday the church is full at 2 a.m. Working people gather to pray intensively for church growth and breakthroughs.

There is no other way to make any progress in the ministry than to work in the realm of the spirit. The Bible says, "Epaphras was always labouring in prayer." The principle of massive organized prayer is what you need to bring about a breakthrough in your ministry.

Epaphras...always labouring fervently for you in prayers, that ye may stand perfect and complete in all the will of God.

Colossians 4:12

There are some people who see me as an administrator and a strategist. Anyone who knows me closely knows that as I write this book, I do not even have a desk or an office. But I do have a study where I pray and I do have places where I spend time praying. There is no shortcut in the ministry. There is no other way than that which has been set by the Lord. There is no other example than that which has been set by Jesus. Peter said that he wanted to give himself to prayer and the Word. Prayer and the Word are more important than administration and strategies!

> But we will give ourselves continually to prayer, and to
> the ministry of the word.
>
> Acts 6:4

14. The principle of using lay people to do the work

One of the great secrets of a large church is in the use of lay people or voluntary church workers. These volunteer workers can do most of the church work.

I have several pastors who are not paid a dime for all of their hard work. The Lord pays them Himself. They work very hard on Sundays and other evenings. They make huge sacrifices in their private lives in order to be pastors and shepherds. Many very big churches use this principle and are succeeding. May the Lord give you understanding and revelation concerning this vital principle.

I am always saddened when I see a small church of one hundred people employing seven full-time pastors. I often ask myself, "How much will one pastor be paid? Do the wives of these pastors work? Do they make enough money to survive?" Such environments are the breeding grounds for discontent and rebellious elements! Many church rebellions are related to money. When money is left out of the ministry, people are able to concentrate on the work of the Lord because they love God.

Many pastors in my church are doing well as lay pastors. If some of them were to come into full-time ministry, things may change. The church may be able to pay them enough money, but they may not be at the stage where they are ready for full-time ministry. New problems relating to salaries and income levels may arise. These problems have the potential to disrupt the work of ministry.

I suggest this to every senior pastor: analyze the church conflicts you have ever had. Aren't most of them related to money? **Make use of unpaid people. They are the key to a peaceful and stable church environment!**

I see a ministry growing! I see your ministry growing! I see you rising up in the Kingdom of God! I see you taking your place! I know the Lord is going to use you! He has determined to use you! The mega church is for you! The anointing is yours! [77]Rise up with wisdom and possess what the Lord has placed before you!